Tips for Carefree Landscapes

Tips for Carefree Landscapes

Over 500 Sure-Fire Ways to Beautify Your Yard and Garden

Marianne Binetti

A Garden Way Publishing book

Storey Communications, Inc.
Pownal, Vermont 05261

Cover design by Nancy Lamb
Text design by Judy Eliason and Leslie Noyes
Cover painting by Brigita Fuhrmann
Illustrations by Brent Cardillo
Edited by Benjamin Watson

The information in this book is true and complete to the best of our knowledge. All recommendations are made without guarantee on the part of the author or Storey Communications, Inc. The author and publisher disclaim all liability incurred with the use of this information.

Printed in the United States by Crest Litho
Third Printing, September 1990

Library of Congress Cataloging-in-Publication Data

Binetti, Marianne, 1956-
    Tips for carefree landscapes : over 500 sure-fire ways to beautify
your yard and garden / Marianne Binetti
       p.   cm.
    "A Garden Way Publishing book."
    ISBN 0-88266-604-5
    ISBN 0-88266-572-3 (pbk.)
    1. Landscape gardening.   I. Title.
SB473.B52   1990
635.9 - - dc20

To my children,
Angela, Tony, and Alisa,
for the roots; and to
my husband, Joe,
for the wings.

Contents

Introduction

Lazy gardeners really can have lovely landscapes. This book will introduce you to a laid-back, relaxed approach to gardening. *Tips for Carefree Landscapes* is written for those people who want to work smarter, not harder in their gardens.

The key to success lies in planning and planting for maximum enjoyment, with minimum maintenance. All gardens require some maintenance, but many homeowners neither enjoy nor have the time for constant upkeep. You hereby have my permission to take shortcuts or even ignore the gardening tasks that you hate to do. The gardening tips included here are designed to save every gardener time and energy. Whether you measure your property in inches or acres, the ideas presented in these pages will teach you gardening the easy way.

I do realize that some people get deep personal satisfaction from keeping a hedge neatly sheared four times a year. Another homeowner may detest any pruning job but enjoy raking leaves each fall, or buying annual flowers every spring. The purpose of this book is to cut down or eliminate outdoor chores that are tedious or strenuous, leaving you more time to delve into whatever aspect of gardening holds more interest for you. Even if you choose to express that interest in a hammock tied between two shade trees.

This book is also written for those poor souls who just hate to garden. If having a yard that the neighbors won't complain about is your only gardening goal, then let me welcome you to the world of carefree landscapes. You can just leave your guilt in the tool shed. Not every homeowner feels the need to gush over pretty flowers or to appreciate a weed-free lawn. A practical majority would just like a yard that looks nice and doesn't tie them down.

There are plenty of gardening fanatics out there who also need this book. If you're a truly devoted rosarian, you may not agree with my minimalist approach to rose care. Instead, you'll be more interested in the tips for lowering lawn maintenance. Why waste time on the lawn when you're dying to devote Saturday mornings to your roses? Even the most dedicated gardener can use a few shortcuts.

Beginning gardeners (and others who don't speak Latin) will appreciate that, in this book, common names are used throughout and common sense prevails.

Plenty of gardening books delve into the nomenclature and detailed descriptions of plant life. This is not one of them. The trees, shrubs, and flowers that are recommended in the following chapters will be easy to look up in reference books if you need more information. Gardening shortcuts, not lengthy plant descriptions, fill these pages.

I just couldn't help throwing in some gardening stories among the tips and charts. My weekly garden column ,"The Compleat Home Gardener," has put me in touch with garden clubs, farmers, city gardeners, and organic enthusiasts alike. My readers helped write this book by sending in tips and shortcuts and evaluating all the low-maintenance ideas I've written about over the years. This is one reason that each chapter ends in a question-and-answer format. These are the questions that my readers ask over and over again. Chances are they're the same questions that pop into your head when you pull on the gardening gloves.

The final chapter features my morbid collection of gardening horror stories. Reading about other people's mistakes somehow makes us relax a little more about our own little blunders.

Tips for Carefree Landscapes preaches a simple, fuss-free approach to gardening. I invite you to enjoy your garden more and worry about it less — don't fight Mother Nature or buck *human* nature. If you do, you'll discover the secret that gardeners have shared since time began — that the blissful peace and paradise of Eden can be as close as your own backyard.

CHAPTER ONE

Landscaping Rules for the Lazy Gardener

If you sincerely want to enjoy the lifestyle of a lazy gardener, then you must memorize and follow the golden rule of lazy gardening: DON'T FIGHT MOTHER NATURE.

There are some dedicated and detail-oriented gardeners who spend a lifetime defying this rule. Perhaps they like the challenge, the constant battle, or maybe they just march to the beat of a rebellious drummer. These are the folks with plenty of free time to spend on a picture-perfect garden.

Then there are the rest of us. Weekend gardeners, or even monthly gardeners, who are short on time and energy but long on vision and ideas. Homeowners who want a great-looking yard — even a beautiful, flower-filled landscape — without the hours of daily maintenance required to care for it.

Joining the ranks of the lazy gardeners doesn't allow you an unmown lawn or knee-high weeds. Start with a landscape plan designed for more free time. Now get ready to adjust your attitude. Lazy gardeners simply work smarter instead of harder. They get the maximum return on a minimum of energy investment. Less work and more to show for it.

The secret is to hire Mother Nature to work your garden on the days when you're just too busy, too forgetful or too... relaxed.

Landscaping Tips That Hire Mother Nature

Choose plants that are native to your area.
This includes the lush wild things that you can transplant from roadsides and wooded lots, as well as the improved hybrids that are relatives of your native plants.

In the mild maritime climate where I garden, there are wild rhododendrons that bloom beautifully with no attention from anyone. Unfortunately, these native rhodies also grow tall and spindly. Plant breeders to the rescue! New hybrid rhododendrons have now been bred with compact growth habits. We still get a shrub that loves the acid soil and wet weather, but new improvements in its size and flowers make growing rhododendrons in mild climates a successful experience for the lazy gardener.

In the Deep South, the high humidity and heavy rainfall support magnolias, palms, and pine trees. Improvements on these native plants have produced more attractive varieties that still tolerate the clay soil and summer heat of that region.

Plant your local nursery's version of these native plants and you'll already have Mother Nature on your side. There's no need to apologize for your soil or climate when the plants you choose already have their ancestral roots buried in your dirt.

The same idea works in the arid Southwest. Heat-loving wildflowers like yucca spring up even in the desert. Why fuss with watering worries for thirsty plants when you can have drought-resistant wildflowers instead? Any plant that survives in the desert will do just as well when ignored in your unwatered garden.

Make the most of what you've got.

Is there a low wet spot in your yard that rots the roots of every plant? Plant a bog garden with moisture-loving lilies, wild irises, and pretty astilbe.

Is the soil dry and rocky out front? Put in a rock garden with gravel-loving alpine plants and sedums.

Too much shade? Plant a woodland garden of ferns and bleeding heart or a more formal display of begonias, lobelia, and hosta.

Does a steep slope or hillside make gardening a terror for you? Turn the terror into terracing and display roses, grapes, or a garden of blooming vines on the site.

Remember that a lazy gardener is not so quick to call in the bulldozer and have property leveled and trees taken down. Work with what you've been given, and Mother Nature may reward you with less maintenance and a more original landscape design.

Repeat your successes.

Most homeowners plant too many different kinds of plants and end up with a confused collection. It makes good design sense to repeat the same trees or shrubs, especially in a formal front-yard design.

If a plant survives happily in your yard, reward it by inviting its brothers and sisters to move in, too.

If your lilac bush blooms beautifully each spring, don't just brag about it — put in a lilac hedge.

If pine trees survive your cold winter winds when everything else is blown to bits, use pines to form a screening hedge.

If you've discovered irises blooming in an overgrown or neglected corner of the yard, then get more irises, or peonies, or whatever it is that blooms in that spot without making any demands on your precious time.

Whatever grows well, plant more of it. You don't need a lot of different kinds of plants as long as the plants you have look great. Professional landscape designers carry this idea to an extreme every time they plan for a groundcover.

Enlist the volunteers.

When something pops up uninvited, don't be so quick to call it a weed. Attractive trees and shrubs are not the only native plants that enhance a garden. Wildflowers and sturdy groundcovers sometimes crash into the garden uninvited, but can turn out to be well-mannered guests that are wildly appreciated.

Now it's time for a story. This tale about a naughty rose garden actually happened. The fellow that wrote in to share the story had been reading my gardening column for years, when suddenly the phrase "Don't Fight Mother-Nature" assumed real meaning in his life.

Once upon a time Mr. Rose (Can you tell that's not his real name?) grew fabulous roses and enjoyed them immensely. He and his family then moved to a new home and took possession of a rather shady backyard. Mr. Rose took his prize rose bushes with him, of course, but they started to behave badly. Black spot and mildew appeared on the foliage and would not leave, no matter how much time and money he invested in sprays. Although roses need plenty of sun and air circulation to keep them disease-free, Mr. Rose simply could not convince his neighbors to cut down the trees that shaded his property.

Well, one morning a fern popped up in the middle of the rose bed. It was a common little fern, the type that seemed to volunteer all over the yard. As the once great rose grower bent down to pull out the offending weed, a light bulb went on in his head. The pouting roses were no longer a joy to grow. But ferns — now here was a plant that might grow happiness.

Little by little the roses were replaced with ferns. All types of ferns from all over the world. Mr. Rose simply replaced his passion for roses with a passion for fern collecting — a marriage of convenience that grew into a blissful union. Divorced from his devotion to the beautiful but temperamental rose, his new life was as peaceful and serene as the shady fern garden.

They all lived happily ever after, or so I assume, since Mr. Rose never wrote again to complain about any fern problems.

Now the morale to that story, in case it slipped by you, is to grow what grows well in your garden. Stop growing the same problem-plagued plants year after year. Roses just happened to be the villain in this story. You may be trying to grow ferns and notice a wild rose plant rambling over. That's your cue to put in a rose garden. When Mother Nature drops a hint about what she would like to grow on your property, pick up on it, and elaborate.

Mulching: The best idea to steal from Mother Nature.

Imagine a product that kills weeds, fertilizes plants, and keeps things watered. There is such a time-saver, and not only is it free for the taking, but some people are even paid to haul it away. This miracle product is mulch.

A mulch is any substance that covers up the soil between plants. The best mulches are compost, bark chips, wood shavings, and pine needles. These are mulches that decay or break down into the soil, fertilizing the plants as they do. By covering the soil with a mulch, you block out weed seeds and seal in moisture. Less weeding and watering. To understand the miracle of mulch, think about the floor of a forest. No soil is visible. The ground is covered with fallen leaves and debris, and yet, through all this mess, a vast assortment of plant life thrives. This is the way nature intended plants to grow. Don't fight it. Cover up the naked soil and you'll be smothering away half your gardening chores. For more mulching details, turn to Chapter Nine.

Tips for Planning without Panic

When faced with a vacant lot or a yard that's full of weeds, most folks do the natural thing and panic before they start to pitch in. Try to get the panic stage over with quickly, so that the scheming and planning can begin.

Draw your plan right on the ground.

Getting a plan down on paper doesn't always require the use of a tape measure and surveying tools. Many times I've designed gardens without measuring an inch. For a small yard or on a newly cleared lot, marking up the ground is quicker and simpler than transferring everything to graph paper. All you need is a sack of flour and a windless day.

Imagine your property as a chalkboard and the kitchen flour as your chalk. Now, rip a hole in the corner of the flour sack and spill a line of flour on the ground, to indicate the shape of the lawn, the lengths and widths of pathways, and the area planned for flowers, shrubs, and trees. Make great big circles with the flour to signify large trees, and small X's to fill in with shrubs or flowers. What you're cooking up is a general plan, to give you an idea of how many plants to buy and what type of square footage you'll be covering with lawn.

The flour won't sit there forever, so take notes or pictures of what you come up with. Now you can pace out the square footage of the lawn you just drew in.

If you're not sure about a design, use a length of hose or heavy rope to mark the shape of lawns and flower beds before you chalk them in.

Daydream your way to a design.

Lazy gardeners will love this comfy-chair, big-window approach to planning. Grab a chair and sit in front of the window that overlooks that ugly area. Now draw. No artistic ability? Great! You won't get bogged down in details. Just scribble down small circles for shrubs and large ones for trees. A big oval is the lawn. Zigzag lines can denote pathways. Nothing to it. You should be getting ideas now and a surge of inspiration. If nothing pops into your head, go stick your nose in a book. There are excellent photographs and diagrams in gardening magazines and landscaping books. Just don't get overly inspired and draw in an excess of high-maintenance flower beds.

This is not the time to worry about specific plant names and varieties. Just write down the shape or color of the plants you envision. Like "low evergreen groundcover" next to the driveway, or "year-round color" next to the front door. Add the words "mini orchard" if you want a bunch of fruit trees and "my favorite plant" if you have a spot that you look at often and a tree or shrub that you've always wanted to own.

When you come to the low, wet spots or hot, dry areas, just pencil them in with a big question mark. You'll need some special plants for these problem areas, and it may take some asking around to find out what they are.

The do-it-yourself design work can either get more detailed or stop at this point. Some homeowners get enthused and enjoy fine-tuning the design as they start to plant according to their personal plan. Others find their true calling is not in landscape planning and decide to conserve energy and frustration by hiring someone else to draw up a design.

Getting Help with a Plan

Call area nurseries to ask about free design services.
Stress your low-maintenance needs. Some nurseries will provide a detailed planting plan as a courtesy when you purchase the plants from them. An experienced nursery person knows what plants are easy to grow and which groups of plants look great together.

If you're clever enough to visit during the slow season or in the midst of a rainstorm, you can corner one of these knowledgeable people at a nursery and pick his or her brains about plants that aren't picky. Now play fair. You should pay for the free advice by patronizing the nursery. You'll soon be recognized as a good customer and get all the gardening information you can handle.

Contact a college in your area that teaches landscaping.
You could offer to give a student experience on your lot, or let your yard be used for a homework project. I can remember my college days at Washington State University, when the horticulture students were required to design a residential landscape from scratch. We worked on real yards that belonged to real people. Real *smart* people, who had volunteered their property for the assignment. We got a grade and they got a free design complete with a plant list.

Pay a call on those people with the most beautiful yard in your neighborhood.
Find out who designed it. Don't act surprised if the owners tell you they did it

themselves. Now go ahead and ask if they'd consider helping you get started with a paper plan for your yard. Even if they decline, you've still just paid them a lovely compliment.

Tips for Working with a Designer

- Be specific and talk freely about the type of landscape you have in mind.

- Make a list of what you want most in your yard. If mowing a lawn or harvesting your own fruit is worth the effort to you, then say so right up front.

- Be firm about what plants you don't like. If you absolutely hate ivy, than refuse to have it in your yard, no matter how perfect it is as a groundcover.

- Ask for substitutes or a second choice if the plants your designer suggests don't grab you. Your home's outside design should be as personalized and well thought out as your interior design — with a lot less upkeep.

Go straight to the top and hire a professional.

Landscape architects are very familiar with low-maintenance garden designs. Many of the commercial buildings and open spaces they design require low maintenance.

Design Ideas That Save on Sweat

Divide the yard into a series of mini gardens.

If you group all of your like plants together, it becomes easier to care for them. That way, all the azaleas that need pruning in June and fertilizing in March are in one section. You can finish your pruning or feeding much faster when you don't have to hunt all over the yard for the plants.

The mini garden concept makes it easier and more efficient for you to spend short blocks of time in the garden. It's convenient to putter around in your "blue garden," for instance, and not get sidetracked by the chores that need to be done in the heather beds. No matter that the blue garden consists of just one blue spruce tree and two plants with blue flowers. Name it the "blue garden" and you've organized a section of the yard in your mind. You may even start collecting more blue-blooming plants once you get a handle on that one corner of the yard.

It's easier to experiment and enlarge your gardening interests when you break up the yard into mini gardens. Replant the rose garden with daylilies, for example, if your roses grow too demanding. (I really don't mean to keep picking on the roses. There are some well-behaved roses that perform wonderfully for lazy gardeners. More about them in Chapter Five.)

Gather plants that need more moisture near the edge of your lawn.
This way, when you set up the sprinkler to keep the lawn from drying up, you'll be watering the thirsty azaleas or chrysanthemums at the same time. Efficiency is the motto of the lazy gardener.

Raise the beds around your lawn and patio.
Use landscaping timbers, stones, or bricks to hold back the soil. Raised beds are easier to weed and look tidy, even when you don't get around to edging the lawn.

Group sprawling, floppy shrubs and flowers away from the house where they can be enjoyed from a distance.
A row of overgrown, blooming shrubbery looks lush as a faraway background across the yard, but up close you see a confused jumble of arching branches — especially offensive if they lose their leaves in winter.

Plant compact, dwarf evergreens near front entries or frequently used paths.
You won't waste time pruning them, and the more formal parts of the garden will have a naturally more refined look.

Avoid messy trees around patios and driveways.
Use trees with small leaves and evergreens that don't shed for patio areas. Be careful of fruiting trees or those with sticky sap and flowers when planting close to entryways. Lazy gardeners hate to sweep patios and paths.

Keep high-labor plants like roses close and convenient.
Next to the driveway or right outside the back door are two suggestions. The idea is to keep the fussy plants constantly in front of your face, so you'll be forced to confront the insect invasion or drinking needs of the plants at once. Plants growing in a hidden side yard or distant corner are often ignored. Keep the demanding plants where their demands can be easily met.

Group plants together in islands or mounds rather than as solitary specimens in your lawn.
Plantings of isolated shrubs and trees make lawn mowing more difficult. Besides, plants look lonely all by themselves, floating adrift in a blue-green sea of lawn.

Tips for More Constructive Construction

Tug it on a tarp.
Once you get into the actual digging and hauling that goes with putting in a new garden bed or yard, you may find yourself depending a lot on a wheelbarrow. Don't

get trapped, get *tarped* instead. Using an old tarp or thick sheet of plastic is easier than lifting for lazy gardeners with lazy backs. Just rake rocks and debris onto the tarp and then drag your refuse away. A tarp works well, too, for dragging heavy bags of peat moss and fertilizer across the lawn. When you add or transplant a new tree or shrub, it will be easier and safer to lift it a few inches onto a tarp than to roll it awkwardly into a tilted wheelbarrow.

Another reason to have a tarp or piece of canvas handy is to keep things tidy during construction. Don't shovel soil onto pathways or the lawn when you dig a hole. Pile up the extra dirt onto the tarp instead.

You'll find the piece of canvas or plastic convenient for raking leaves, too. Instead of fumbling with garbage sacks that take four hands to hold open and fill, just rake your leaf piles onto the tarp and drag them away to a corner of the garden to rot. Use the same idea when you find yourself pulling weeds. It's much easier to toss the weeds over your shoulder onto a large tarp than to fill buckets with weeds and lug them all over the yard.

Boulders can be rolled onto a strong piece of canvas and then pulled to a permanent resting place. Particularly if your property is sloped or terraced, you'll find dragging a tarp around a lot easier than maneuvering something on wheels.

Farm out the labor to others.

Hire a bulldozer for the really big jobs like leveling the land or putting in a driveway.

Rent the right stuff.

If you're comfortable with large, noisy machines, then consider renting one of the metal monsters for an afternoon. Use the yellow pages to call rental outlets and ask about the availability of "bobcats" or "rock hounds" or powerful tillers to chew up the ground. A bobcat is just a mini bulldozer and can be used to do final grading or to clear weeds and brambles from an area. A rock hound is a motorized riding machine that tills the soil and collects the rocks in a large wire basket.

Good tools can also be rented, along with seed spreaders, lawn rollers, and electric hedge trimmers. Most of the heavy-duty work needs to be done only once, so renting rather than buying the proper equipment will appeal to the frugal gardener.

Throw a party.

Work parties work out well, so long as you state up front that some goal needs to be met. Instead of saying, "Come on over to work in our yard," offer a more specific invitation:

> HELP! WE MUST GET OUR LAWN IN BEFORE WINTER
> AND WE HAVE 5,000 SQUARE FEET TO HOE AND RAKE!
> BRING TOOLS AND WORK UP A HEARTY APPETITE FOR
> A CELEBRATION SUPPER AT SUNSET.

Now you have offered a challenge along with an invitation, and everyone knows you'll party at sunset once the goal is met.

An etiquette tip is in order here. You don't invite casual acquaintances to work parties. The only exception would be neighbors who are also putting in a new yard and can invite you to a work party in return.

Support your favorite charity.
Not everyone wants to impose on friends and family to do their dirty work. You can still haul in a work crew and get some satisfaction out of paying for the service. Look into hiring a club or team for a flat fee. High school clubs and athletic teams that sponsor car washes and pancake feeds may be interested in giving you a couple of hours labor in exchange for a donation. Choose a time-consuming project like spreading and raking topsoil or hauling rocks or bricks to the construction site. Be prepared to supervise, and make sure everyone knows exactly what is expected of them and how much the group will earn.

Put your kids to work.
Don't overlook child labor if you happen to have a healthy crop of kids to exploit. If your offspring would rather stare at the television than play pioneer family and help put in a yard, you'll have to hoodwink them into service with incentives.

Creative Incentives to Get Kids Working

■ Announce that the entire family is going to the movies or out for pizza or whatever else gets children's adrenaline flowing. Since our own three kids are still small, the promise of a popsickle has always been enough to get them motivated. Just stress that the fun will begin as soon as the work is done and dangle that carrot to motivate the muscles.

■ Try getting them to give their personal best by personalizing the chores. Mark off the yard into sections with string. Assign weeding or raking by the quadrant to each child. Use flour to write the names of each little laborer on the soil and then tell the kids there's a project waiting outside with their name on it.

■ Pay kids by the job, not by the hour. This way the fast worker will be rewarded and the dawdlers will learn the hard way.

■ Work alongside your youngsters and tell a story as you weed or hoe. Stop the story when they stop working. Personalize the story to keep things interesting for little kids, or try a suspenseful ghost tale for older children.

■ If you've got moody teenagers, harness those hormones by putting them to work. Give them a chance to air complaints and tell you everything you're doing wrong. Promise not to interrupt as long as they keep working and show progress in either the gardening or the discussion. If things really get heated, switch to a gardening chore that takes hoeing or digging. These therapy sessions in the garden mean you can root out dissension while you root out the dandelions. Sow seeds of communication along with the carrots. Keep rebellion in check as well as the rose hedge. Just don't get close to the pruning shears when a heated discussion develops. Your job is to listen, not to lecture — it keeps them working longer.

■ Bring an alarm clock out to the yard. Give everyone in the family a different job and, when the alarm goes off, everybody rotates jobs.

Don't fight human nature.
Kids seek out positive reinforcement and avoid negative reinforcement. Make gardening fun for them. Avoid the term "yard work" and invite your offspring to join you in the garden. Praise them for even attempting to help you. Act as if seeding a new lawn or watering a shrub is a sacred task, an honor that only the privileged can enjoy. Just as Tom Sawyer suckered his friends into painting Aunt Polly's fence, your own offspring can be conned into doing the gardening chores you're too busy to attend to.

A word of caution about kids and power lawn mowers. If your teenagers are too young to drive a car, they're probably too young to operate a power mower. See Chapter Two for a safer alternative to dangerous power mowers.

Arranging the Plants while Arranging for Laziness

Plant in groups of like plants.
Once again, take a cue from Mother Nature. Ferns are arranged in clumps and colonies in the wild. Daisies crowd together for comfort in the field. Wild foxgloves

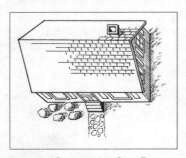

Figure 1: Plant a group of small shrubs close together to get the mature look of a larger plant.

reseed themselves in large families so they can nod amicably to one another in the wind. Plants look happy and content amongst their relatives. A single specimen plant is fine as an accent or to anchor a clump of spreading plants, but have a heart for the wee little plants that look lost as singles. Clump them together and notice how much more confidence they seem to have.

Here's an easy way to fill in the vastness of a vacant lot and not have an overgrown jungle in a few years.

First, buy young shrubs in multiples of

three, five, or seven.

Clump the shrubs close together to get the mature look of a larger plant, and to give you large patches of something green and growing.

In a year or two, when the shrubs start to look crowded, you can snatch away the middle shrubs and use them to landscape the side or back yard that you never got around to fixing up. (See illustrations.) Why is this easier than just buying and planting one large plant? (I knew you'd ask.) The reason is that finding large shrubs at a reasonable price entails a lot more work than locating three starter plants in gallon-sized containers. The payoff really comes a couple years down the road, when the little shrubs have doubled in size and you have your own nursery stock to finish landscaping the rest of the yard.

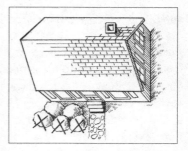

Figure 2: When the shrubs begin to look crowded, remove some of them to open up the space.

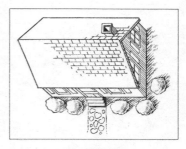

Figure 3: Transplant the shrubs you've removed in other parts of the landscape.

Try this design formula for filling in a planting area:
- 5 to 7 low-growing plants
- 3 medium-height plants
- 1 tall focal-point plant

The five to seven small plants should all be the same type and variety, and should hug the ground. An example would be dwarf heather or creeping juniper.

The three medium plants should be taller and more bushy than the small plants, but not as tall as the focal-point plant that you choose. Think of three evergreen azaleas or three dwarf mugho pines.

The tall accent plant doesn't really have to be towering, so long as it stands out and is distinctive from the other two plant groups. A Japanese laceleaf maple or a small flowering tree would do the job.

Now set the tall accent plant in the center or off to the side a bit in the planting bed. Group the three medium shrubs below it, or off to the side, to balance the height of the tall focal-point plant. Fill in with the low-growing plants spaced evenly throughout the planting area. (See illustration on next page.)

When using this method you can choose a season or theme for each area that gets planted. One area can feature plants that bloom in spring. Another corner might consist of tall, medium, and low-growing plants that all sport colorful fall foliage. If you want evergreens, choose varieties that contrast with one another. You aren't limited to basic green when it comes to choosing shrubs.

Of course, you can also use this formula in larger areas by adding more tall focal-point plants, then increasing the number of medium-sized plants for balance and filling in with even more of the low-growing, ground-hugging plants.

Plant something else besides just a plant.

If you've got a large area that needs planting, don't get carried away and fill in every bit with living plants. Landscaping for the lazy gardener includes boulders or garden accents in the place of tall plants. Fallen logs or tree stumps in the place of shrubs, and — the best friends that any lazy yard owner could have — rocks. Lots and lots of rock and pebbles.

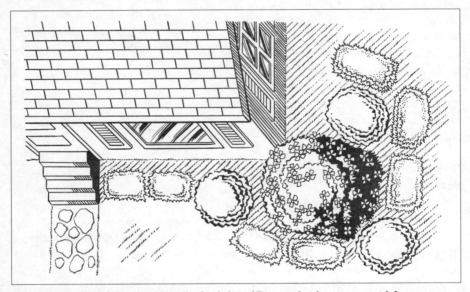

Group three medium shrubs around a taller focal plant, filling out the planting area with five to seven low-growing plants.

Rock, Stone and Gravel Gardening — Solid Ideas for No Maintenance

Rocks don't die. Boulders don't need water, and a bed of gravel has never yet needed a mowing or pruning job. There are no rocks in your head if you plan for more rocks in the garden.

Even purist plant lovers will have to admit that the smooth surface of a boulder is perfect for enhancing the rough texture of an evergreen, and the light gray color of a gravel bed helps display the bright colors from the blooming flowers behind it. But don't take my word for it. Take a look at the designs of Mother Nature. Alpine scenes of spectacular beauty with jagged boulders amongst the flowers. Ferns and fronds hanging happily over the gravel in a streambed. Rock-solid proof that gardening with stones is what nature intended. Now, let's get creative with rocks.

Group three large boulders around a focal-point tree.

You must plant the boulders as you would a shrub. Dig a hole and bury at least a third of the rock, so it looks natural. If this idea sounds like it's been borrowed from a Japanese garden, you're right. Rocks take on deep symbolism in Japanese gardens, and you can certainly invent your own inner meanings as you plant and position your personal supply of boulders. The rocks in our yard represent a different planet or life form each time somebody new asks about them. Some of them even represent that we were too lazy to move them from their natural resting place. (See illustration.)

Partially buried rocks create a natural-looking setting for a tall accent plant.

■ Border your planting beds with a strip of gravel six inches to one foot wide. Use an edging of landscaping timbers or larger rocks to keep any gravel from spilling onto the lawn.

■ Put in a pool of pebbles for a refreshing relief from lawn and shrubs. Just dig a small shallow pit about four inches deep. Line the depression with plastic and fill with smooth pebbles or large river stones. Now edge the pool with large flat stones and have a wonderful time planting around the edge. (See illustration.)

To create a pebble pool, fill a shallow pit with pebbles, then edge the pool with large flat stones.

■ If you've got lots of rocks and stones, use them for paving your paths. Lay them level in a bed of sand if you want to get fancy. Or go for a cobblestone look and set them in cement if you really want to keep weeds from coming up through the cracks.

■ Don't try lifting large stones into a wheelbarrow when moving them about. Use that piece of canvas I lectured you about and drag your rocks away.

■ Wash your homegrown rocks. They'll look more like the expensive rocks that the professionals use once you get the dirt off. Scrub your boulders with a stiff brush and hose them down before you pronounce them a garden highlight. Our toddlers enjoyed a whole summer washing rocks for us in their kiddie pool.

■ Rake the rocks right out of your soil to use as gravel. Throw them onto a screen for washing and sorting.

■ If you aren't lucky enough to own rocky soil, don't despair. There is hope for you poor souls with stoneless soil and a pebble-free existence. Beg a few boulders from the folks living up on the hill. Go for a drive and look for some lonely stones. The highway department is sometimes kind enough to post signs alerting you of rocks nearby. This is prime rock-hunting territory, where friendly boulders will throw themselves over cliffs and roll right down to your car. Who can resist such assertive stones? Although you do need permission to gather plants off public lands, I've never heard of rock thieves doing hard time. Unless you plan on knocking off a rock quarry, that is.

■ Learn the rocky lingo and exploit it. A one-man rock is one that one man could carry. A two-man rock is twice as large. Most one-man rocks could be considered boulders. There are also one-woman rocks and child-sized rocks. Always gather one-man rocks if you're a woman, and always bring at least one man with you. Point out that, since it's one-man rocks you're after, a man will have to lift and carry them, not a woman.

If you are male, bring another fellow along and exclaim over a bigger-than-average one-man rock. Be sure to call it a two-man rock by mistake. Most macho men feel bound by some inner code of honor to carry that stone to the ends of the earth without any help. Few men can resist proving that they can carry a two-man rock all by themselves.

Ten Ways to Add Character to Your Yard without Adding Work

Get creative with things that don't die. Landscape designers call these "garden features" or "non-living focal points". Things like birdbaths, sundials, and large boulders can add charm, but not any more work, to your garden design. Anything that doesn't have to be fed, watered, or pruned should be of interest to the lazy gardener. Now, don't get carried away. A flock of pink flamingos or a lineup of ceramic dwarfs could detract more than they add to your yard's character. Use restraint and avoid garish colors, unless you plan to advertise a roadside carnival. Borrow these classic ideas for garden accents:

1. Clean up with a birdbath or sundial in the spot where nothing seems to survive. A hot, dry area close to the house where the lawn refuses to grow is one likely place. Surround the feature with gravel edged in brick or stone. Add pots of geraniums or sun-loving marigolds for summer color.

2. A protruding tree stump doesn't have to be offensive. Add a mound of topsoil around the stump so low evergreen plants can surround it. Now set a birdhouse or bird feeder on the stump. A wooden planting box filled with summer flowers would also turn that stump into a pedestal.

3. Fancy up your walkways. Set clay-colored stepping stones in a bed of gray gravel. Edge a cement path with bricks. Line a bark path with large rocks. Just make sure every gravel or bark pathway has a layer of plastic or similar weed-blocking material underneath it. No lazy gardener wants to be (perish the thought) pulling weeds from a path.

4. Surround a large tree with a circular bench. Stop fighting with Mother Nature and trying to force grass to grow where it has no business growing. An old-fashioned circular bench gives you a cool spot to relax during your lazy spells.

5. Add an arch or arbor — no plants are required. If you already have a fence, then match the arch to the style of the fence. Any spot that has a gate can be embellished with an archway. A garden arbor can be small or large, built right off the house or freestanding in the garden. An arch or an arbor will give you height and a focal point in the yard without the pruning and fussing required for a small tree. Don't think only English Country-style homes can host archways. A straight and simple design will complement the clean lines of modern architecture. You can always add the climbing roses or flowering vines later on in life if you get a spurt of energy.

6. Budget for a bench and you'll give your garden an instantly peaceful look. We're not talking plastic patio furniture here. A garden bench should be made of stone or rot-resistant wood so it can sit out all year long. (Lazy gardeners don't like to store away furniture.) Replicas of the classic wrought iron and wood park bench are now very affordable. Prepare a spot with cement blocks, bricks, or just plain gravel spread over black plastic as a weed block. Set the bench on this mini patio in a spot where you can view the scene even from inside the house. You've just created a pleasing garden scene that won't wilt when it's ignored. You may even be inspired enough to add some tall flowers to bloom behind the bench, or a clump of fragrant plants alongside it. Adding a bench may encourage you to sit a spell and enjoy the privileges of being a lazy gardener.

7. Add a stream without the water. A dry streambed can be made with rocks and plastic. Dig a shallow ditch in the shape of a wiggling snake. Lay down plastic. Fill in with gravel. Then edge with large rocks and medium-sized stones. You'll never have to weed or water in that area again. Just don't make the mistake of adding running water to your streambed. Water gardens drown their owners in extra work.

8. Gaze upon a gazebo, instead of a flower garden. The return of the gazebo to American landscapes signals the rise of us lazy gardeners. Even a small gazebo or summerhouse takes up plenty of room, adds height and dimension, and requires a fraction of the maintenance that a large flower garden or shrub border would demand. Order a kit or build it yourself, but try to go rustic and avoid all that painting. If you think gardening is work, wait until you spend a day painting Victorian bric-a-brac.

9. Pave the problem with a courtyard. Steal this idea from Spain, where the lack of rain makes growing a lawn impossible. You don't have to keep your patio in the backyard. Pave your problems away in the front yard by adding a low wall and potted plants for a more formal look. A front courtyard is not only gracious and welcoming, but it frees you from mowing as well.

10. Design away work with a deck. Build decks of different levels with steps that connect, or a large deck with eating area, hot tub corner, and storage benches. Garden in containers there, without the bugs and slugs that slither up from the soil.

The Top Ten Landscaping Questions

Q. *We are building our own home on a wooded lot. What can we tell the bulldozing crew that will help us with landscaping later?*
A. The nicest thing a bulldozer can do is scrape off the topsoil and pile it off to the side in a safe place. That way, the excavation work and heavy equipment won't compact the topsoil into hard cement. Mark all the trees you want to save and wrap their trunks in heavy cardboard if equipment will be working close to them. Notice where the masons and cement workers leave their piles of lime and cement. Mortar and cement crumbs will damage plants, so clean them up before you have the topsoil spread and the final grading done on the lot.

Q. *Our lot is not level. There is a level spot near the house, but most of the backyard slopes down to the property line. There is really no way to bring in heavy equipment to add fill. How can we landscape such a yard?*
A. Landscape a sloping yard with several decks and terracing. Extend a deck off the level area close to the front with steps winding down to the next level area of lawn, and maybe a third area for flowering shrubs and an evergreen screen. Terrace a sloping lot by digging into the hillside and using the soil you remove from the first terrace to fill in for the level area of the second terrace. Now cover the sloping areas with groundcover plants to stabilize the hill. Consult a professional when moving large amounts of earth.

Q. *I have a bald spot in my yard. Nothing seems to grow below my large fir trees.*
A. Why should anything want to grow under a large tree? Too much shade and too little water is the double jeopardy that scares off any respectable plant. You can solve the problem neatly by edging the barren area with a circle of brick or stone and then filling in the circle with a bark or gravel mulch. Get fancy if you want and garden in containers or hang baskets of shade-loving plants from the branches. If you really want to plant something beneath the spreading branches, then add at

least three inches of topsoil and choose a shade-loving, drought-resistant groundcover like pachysandra or ivy.

Q. *I want a fast-growing, very narrow hedge to use as a barrier alongside my driveway. It must remain green all year long and not have a root system that would break up my cement drive.*
A. What you want is a "fedge," not a hedge. Start by putting in a chain-link fence alongside the driveway. (Okay, if you can't afford the real thing, put in some fence posts with wire fencing strung between the posts.) Plant ivy all along the fence line and help the first young vines cling to the wire supports. In a short time your fence will be covered with ivy and, instead of pruning, you'll just have to reroute any stray ivy vines back to the wire. Ivy is a lazy gardening classic, but any hardy vine can be trained along a wire fence to form a skinny fedge. Think of it as a living fence that never needs painting. Once it matures, your vine may need a yearly haircut to keep it under control.

Q. *Help! We have a new house, a small budget, and a large lot with absolutely no landscaping. Not a single tree or blade of grass. The weeds are starting to grow all around us, but we need some direction as to priorities. Do trees go in first or a lawn? What about shrubs? We plan on doing all of the work ourselves but don't have much time to do it.*
A. Grass seed to the rescue! Rake the rocks and debris from the lot and then sprinkle grass seed everywhere. Either pray hard for two weeks of rain or invest in a hose and spray attachment to keep the seeds watered. If this is all you get done the first year, then at least you've kept down the weeds by mowing the "lawn" every now and then. The following year you can plan out the shapes of the flower beds and the locations of trees and lawn. You may need to haul in topsoil and work on the quality of your lawn later on when you're not so overwhelmed. Your sparse first year lawn will not go to waste, though. It can be tilled into the soil as a conditioner, and its growth (or lack of it) can tell you a lot about the low spots, dry spots, and hard-to-grow spots in your yard.

Q. *What can we plant for some quick privacy from our neighbors? Our backyard is like being in a fishbowl.*
A. If you feel like a fish out of water and need instant privacy, then put up a fence. Most plants that grow super fast such as a laurel hedge become high-maintenance monsters that need frequent pruning to keep them under control. Try for a more natural look by screening your yard with a mix of trees, shrubs, and fencing. Use a maple tree in one corner with some tall evergreen shrubs around it for low screening, and a pine or other evergreen tree to block out the other corner. A row of flowering shrubs intermixed with hardy evergreens can fill the space between the trees. You can now get away with less fence by just using it between the two trees as a background for the shrubs. (See illustration on next page.) This is the

time to choose a wood fencing material that will weather naturally and skip the painting.

Q. *We moved into a yard that is already landscaped, and have no idea what to call these trees and shrubs that are growing all around our home. How do we find out what plants we have and what special care they need?*

A. To identify mystery plants, snip a sample from a branch that shows leaves, stem, and any fruits or flowers. Then take the evidence to the neighborhood nursery. Most nursery owners are very good at playing Sherlock Holmes and can also tell you how to care for prize specimens.

Q. *When can I prune my overgrown trees and shrubs? They are blocking the light from my windows and barricading pathways.*

A. Prune overly ambitious shrubbery at any time of year. It's pretty hard to kill overgrown shrubs with the pruning shears, but pretty easy to butcher all the beauty out of them. Remove no more than a third of the plant at a time. Don't be afraid to tear out rebellious shrubs that block windows and paths. Constant pruning is not for lazy gardeners, and shrubbery that tries to take over the yard should be banished, not fussed over. Substitute one of the cheerful dwarf evergreens instead. Dwarf varieties may cost more, but they have no ambitions about blocking windows and don't require constant haircuts to keep them in fashion.

Q. *When can I transplant the shrubs in my yard? I need to move some evergreen shrubs and also some flowering bushes.*

A. Make moving day as painless as possible by performing the operation while the patient is asleep. Winter is when outdoor plants go dormant, and as long as the ground is not frozen you can transplant from late fall to early spring. Of course, every gardener has success stories about the time when they just had to move a lilac in full bloom or a rhododendron in the middle of an August heat wave. It is possible to transplant shrubs at any time of the year and have them live to bloom and you to brag about it. The secret is to prepare the new home with a large hole and plenty of good soil. Next, you must commit yourself to faithful watering until new roots can grow. The lazy way is to form a ridge of soil around the new root zone and then lay the hose end in the middle of the plant. Turn on a tiny trickle of water and let it drip slowly into the soil for several hours. If the plant still looks sad after a week of the water treatment, prune back a third of the top growth and wait until spring. Lots of "dead" transplants are reborn the following spring.

Q. *Where can I find some of the plants I read about? I want to put in a few out-of-the-ordinary plants, but everything I see for sale looks just like what everybody else has in their yard. I have read about some easy-care groundcovers and blooming shrubs that should grow in our area, but nobody seems to be selling them locally.*
A. Go plant hunting early in the spring when the selection is at its peak. Try small specialty nurseries rather than chain-store outlets. Ask and you may receive. Most nursery owners are happy to get you any plant you desire if you follow these rules:

1. Write down the common and Latin name of your wish plant and give it to the nursery manager or owner.

2. Order in the fall or winter if you want the plant for spring planting.

3. Put down a deposit to prove you're serious about buying the plant if it can be found.

Don't be too stubborn to change your mind if an experienced nursery grower claims there's a problem growing a certain variety. You don't want to add a demanding prima donna to your yard and then watch it pout around for the next couple of years. No matter how lovely it looks in a picture book, no plant deserves space in your garden if you have to fight with Mother Nature to keep it alive.

CHAPTER TWO

Lawn Care for the Very Lazy

The perfect lawn has become an American obsession. Every homeowner wants a deep green lawn free of weeds and clover and kept as short and uniform as a new pile carpet. The suburban dream of a perfect lawn has created a high-maintenance nightmare. It's time to apologize to dear Mother Nature and wake up from this impossible dream.

The all-American, all-uniform, and always perfect lawn is not a natural phenomenon. Uniform fields of grass are contrary to what Mother Nature had in mind when she planted that first prairie of waving grass and wildflowers. If you plan to enjoy gardening, then remember your pledge not to fight Mother Nature. Stop the conquering and start cooperating. Free yourself from turf-care torture by realizing the evils of the perfect lawn.

The Sinful Side of a Perfect Lawn — A Glutton for your Time, Money, and Energy

Here are three reasons to stop striving for a perfect lawn:

1. *It's a time-consuming task.*
If you stop mowing long enough to think about it, would any lazy gardener waste time on a tree or shrub that demanded weekly pruning? Mowing the perfect lawn is without a doubt the most time-consuming part of owning a patch of grass. The problem stems from the fact that the image of the "perfect lawn" in many neighborhoods is a shortly cropped lawn. A lawn that barely skims the one inch mark on a ruler. Some lawn fanatics will waste time mowing twice a week to achieve this close-cropped look.

These lawn-lovers need to lighten up and lengthen their lawn along with their free time. A supershort lawn consumes more water, more fertilizer, and — worst of all — more time to keep it healthy.

2. *You're wasting energy on weeds.*
Vowing to keep every weed out of your lawn is the fastest way to break a promise. Commit yourself to a weed-free lawn and you'll be wasting precious energy on a

treadmill task. Energy that could be better spent working with your more grateful, more productive, and more beautiful flowers and shrubs.

3. *Money is the root of all evil in maintaining the perfect lawn.*
Maintaining the perfect lawn requires large amounts of water and fertilizer. Not only are water and lawn fertilizers expensive and time-consuming to apply, but this overindulgence on your lawn may come at the expense of the rest of your garden. A greedy lawn demanding constant chemicals and special equipment to keep it near perfection is an enormous burden on any gardening budget.

English estate gardens were once surrounded by luxuriously perfect lawns. This is where Americans got the idea for lots of lawn. English royalty could afford professional gardeners and a grandiose grass budget. The question is, can you?

The perfect lawn is a lot of work. It's high time for lazy gardeners to revolt. Let's reform the rest of the world while we're at it.

The Joys of the Good-Enough Lawn — Flowers, Clover, and Free Time

Free flowers.
Allowing an assortment of volunteer grasses and blooming wildflowers in your lawn provides extra color. A weed is just a plant that grows where it isn't wanted. Tell yourself you really don't mind dandelions — they're edible, you know, so inform the neighbors you're growing them as a salad crop. Tiny blue flowers and white daisies might also volunteer if you let the grass grow a bit longer. A lovely flower garden that will coexist peacefully amidst the grass. By simply adjusting your attitude, you can save yourself acres of money and pick armloads of wildflowers.

Comfy clover.
Rolling in clover has always meant good things. Why work so hard condemning clover? It smells good when it's freshly cut, it stays low, and it keeps its green color all summer long, even when the rest of the lawn is turning brown from lack of water. Clover growing also gives the kids something to do on a summer day. Send them searching for a four-leaf clover and wish them luck.

A better background.
The good-enough lawn doesn't hog the limelight. Your flowers get to be the star attraction. The lawn becomes a background for your lovely trees and blooming plants rather than the formal focal point of your yard, with its every blade in place. A more relaxed lawn means that a few sprawling plants or faded flower petals won't look out of place. Your home will look like it's nestled cozily in a garden — not perched stiffly on a golf course.

I realize that some of you will never be convinced of the joys of the good-enough lawn. If you're the type that gazes on a lawn and instantly sees the weeds instead of the grass, I sympathize. If the first thing you see are bare spots rather than green acres, I understand. If a good-enough lawn will never be good enough for you, then really and truly I do have compassion for your plight. I may not condone your unhealthy obsession, but I do have a confession to make. I am married to a Lawn Perfectionist. My husband may be practically perfect in every other respect, but when it comes to our lawn, his perfectionism turns him into a turf-tending fanatic. He is the Lawn Ranger, always on grass patrol. He cannot see the garden because the lawn gets in his way.

There are millions of homeowners suffering from the obsessive condition of Lawn Perfectionism. Most of them are male. This chapter is for those lawn fanatics who desperately long to be cured.

Now, let's first work out a compromise between the impossible demands of the perfect lawn, and the leisure-time leanings of the lazy gardener. Dig deep into the mind of a lawn perfectionist and you'll find a lazy gardener, lurking inside and longing for the return of leisure.

Getting Down to the Grass Roots with Good Soil

The better the soil, the better the lawn.
If you're putting in a new lawn, then here's your chance to save yourself years of work. Spend time and money now and you'll be paid back with a lawn that requires less watering and fertilizing for the rest of its life.

Good soil means deep soil.
Even if you don't need to haul in topsoil (and many people don't), use a tiller or plow to really break up the soil to a depth of at least twelve inches. This will encourage the grass roots to reach deep into the soil. The deeper the roots, the more water and food they can grab on their own. Shallow-rooted lawns are dependent on their owners for nourishment, since they've never been trained to hunt deep and take care of themselves.

Topsoil shouldn't just sit on top.
If you pay for rich, dark soil, don't just plop it onto your hard-packed ground. The grass seed you plant will want to send roots down only as deep as your topsoil layer. Mix that two inches of topsoil into the top six inches of subsoil. Don't allow a rich top layer to tempt your grass into a shallow and wasteful existence.

Choosing a good topsoil shouldn't be a mystery.
When you buy topsoil, the quality varies greatly. A soil mix with too much sawdust

or undecomposed matter may be low in nitrogen, giving you a yellow lawn. A soil mix heavy in fresh manure may burn tender new grass. Solve the mystery of finding the best soil for your new lawn by calling the nearest sod grower. The professional grass growers in your area will know what type of soil mix is best for your part of the country. They will also know who sells the best grass-growing soil mix. Laziest gardeners take note: While you've got the sod people on the phone, find out what it would cost to sod your new lawn. A new lawn from rolls of sod is instant and easy. You'll still need well-prepared soil, but you won't have anywhere near the watering and weeding hassles of seeding a lawn. This sod carpet of green perfection is going to cost you more. For a small lawn, it's definitely worth it.

A few rocks won't hurt anything.
Don't worry about removing any rocks smaller than a golf ball below the surface of the soil. A generous supply of small rocks below the surface insures good drainage and a healthier lawn.

Use a plank to smooth over rough spots before you plant.
Dragging a board across your newly raked seedbed will even out the bumps and dips. A fun way to do this is to attach a rope at either end of the board. Now weight down the center with a kid or two. As two adults grab the ropes and drag the board, the kids get a ride. Your family can enjoy "dirt surfing" and level the ground at the same time. (See illustration.)

The back of a rake works better for leveling soil than the tines of a rake.
Here's a guaranteed way to cut your raking time in half. Rent or buy a "landscapers rake" also called a "cement finisher's rake." This rake is lightweight but twice as

wide as a standard rake. Lets you rake more ground in less time.

Starting a New Lawn From Seed

Let's get the bad news over with first. There's no real shortcut for starting a lawn from seed. After preparing the soil and sowing the seed, you must commit yourself to keeping the seedbed constantly moist for several weeks. Dry soil is the most common cause of seeding disaster. Console yourself with the thought of all the money you're saving. Sprinkling seed is still the cheapest way to start a new lawn.

Don't skimp on grass seed.
The most expensive grass seeds are the newer named varieties that have been bred for better performance and disease resistance. These hybrid seeds cost more but are definitely worth it to the lazy gardener. For example, instead of reading "perennial ryegrass," the label on the package of seed should bear the name of a named variety, such as "Manhattan perennial ryegrass."

Use a pre-mixed combination of grass types.
Don't plant a lawn of all bluegrass or all ryegrass in an attempt for a unified look. Increase your odds of at least one of the grasses doing well by planting for some ethnic variety. A segregated lawn of just one type of seed is more susceptible to total wipeout from insects or disease.

Don't use up all your seed the first time you plant. Save out some seed for going over the bare spots later on.

Watering the Well-Behaved Lawn

The best friend a lazy gardener could have is an automatic underground sprinkler system. The new sprinkler systems available now are easy to install yourself, since they're put together with plastic pipe and glue instead of heavy metal pipes and a wrench. If you're putting in a new lawn, then adding an automated watering system is definitely the route to relaxation.

Time for a true testimonial to sprinkler systems. I did not always approve of the idea. I am a recent sprinkler system convert, forced into trying the system by the lawn fanatic I'm married to.

When my husband (the Lawn Ranger) suggested we install an underground sprinkler system to water the lawn, I was horrified. Such an extravagant, water-wasting gadget, all for the sake of our greedy lawn. No practical, down-to-earth gardener would stand for such extravagance. Especially since we live near Seattle, the umbrella capital of the world!

But a true lawn fanatic will not listen to reason, and soon my husband dug himself into this project with pick, shovel, and enthusiasm. After several hours, his enthusiasm waned as the size of the rocks in our ground increased. But hope and the dream of a perfect lawn springs eternal. The Lawn Ranger threw in the trowel (along with the pick) and borrowed a tractor. With a gallant "Heigh-ho, Silver, away!" he and the tractor dug ditches all over the lawn in a couple of hours. Assembling the plastic pipes that would carry the water was like joining together a giant Tinker toy.

To my great delight, this episode had a happy ending. Forget the fact that our lawn looks lush, uses less chemical fertilizer, and sprouts fewer weeds. We also waste less water and don't have hoses and sprinklers to trip over. But what really sold me on the watering system was the happier disposition of our other plants. From the roses to the rhododendrons, every plant that first summer resisted insects and disease with remarkable vigor. For years I'd always thought I'd done a good job watering the garden during dry spells. Now I realize how drought-stressed my plants really were. The deeper soaking that the sprinkler system delivered taught me that hand watering and moving around above-ground sprinklers is just not enough. Scientific research backs up what my plants have shown me. If you let a plant suffer stress from dry soil, even once, that plant will have a weakened defense from attacking insects and invading diseases. Just like people, plants are more susceptible to health problems when they are stressed. Keep them watered and you avoid a lot of other problems.

If you're forgetful as well as lazy, then an underground sprinkler system that can be programmed to come on automatically is a plant saver. If your lawn has different water needs from your flowers and shrubs, you can program the system to water the lawn only. Less plant stress means less feeding and spraying and fussing with your plants. A nice little side effect is the lush green lawn.

The cost of installing our watering system was surprisingly low, but then we installed it ourselves. (Okay, leave out the "we" — my husband installed it without my help.) The hassle of digging up our lawn to lay the plastic pipes could have been avoided had we hired the job out. There are slit trenchers that make thin slits in your established lawn. A lawn grows over any scars quickly and full recovery is swift.

If you're a lawn fanatic with a lot of grass, then go ahead and splurge on a sprinkler system. The best place to get more information is from the makers of these systems. Toro and Rainbird are two nationally known manufacturers. Your lawn will not only stay greener, but the rest of the garden will be healthier and less demanding, too.

Bury Your Hose for a Lazier Summer

If the deluxe underground sprinkler system of your dreams is not a reality, then improvise with a simple alternative. Run your garden hose over to that sunny slope or side lawn that is always thirsty. Keep the hose hidden by running it alongside the edge of the lawn bordering the flowerbed. Now cover that hose. A half-inch topping of bark or soil is enough to hide a hose. Leave enough uncovered hose at the end so you can pull it out of hiding when watering is necessary. Just a foot or two coiled up under a shrub, easy to drag out when you need it. Better yet, leave the sprinkler hooked up to the hose and hide the whole unit behind a low shrub, close to the lawn. The incognito hose maneuver will save you the job of coiling and uncoiling the hose all summer. (Yes, I know a true lazy gardener would just leave the hose lying out on the lawn all summer, but this leaves dead marks on the grass.)

Now, what about access from the faucet while this hose stays hooked up? Screwing a hose on and off a faucet all summer is a waste of motion for us lazy gardeners. Eliminate the irritation by attaching a double-headed Siamese faucet head to your outlet. These exotic-sounding faucets are cheap and easy to find at any hardware store. Put one on every faucet. Now you can still fill water cans or attach a second hose for filling the pool or watering the dog. Meanwhile, the buried hose stays in place all summer long, ready to deliver water with a minimum of hassle.

Use a big sprinkler.
The oscillating sprinkler is best for the lazy gardener because the back-and-forth action of this sprinkler will cover a lot of area. Be sure to run it at full force, so that the water will reach the flowers and shrubs that border your lawn as well. Since you're going to water, you might as well water everything within reach.

Water deep — and water less often.
If you're going to go to all the trouble of turning on a watering system, then, for your lawn's sake, water deep. Let the sprinkler run until the top three to four inches of soil are saturated. That way you won't have to think about watering again for days or even weeks. Less frequent but deep watering is not only easier for the lazy lawn grower, but it's better for the health of your lawn. Remember those deep-searching roots we talked about? If you water shallowly, the roots will remain close to the surface, trained to expect their frequent fix of water. But water deep, letting the sprinkler remain on until the water soaks down half a foot or more, and those roots will follow the moisture way down to the depths of your earth. Once down deep, those grass roots will figure out how to extract moisture from the soil on their own and leave you in peace to lie in the sun all summer. The longer you water, the longer you can go without watering again. Some soils need watering overnight to saturate them. In other neighborhoods two hours of watering may be enough. Jab a knife into your soil. If the top three inches aren't dark with moisture, keep on watering.

Deciding when to water.
Don't waste water. It really offends Mother Nature, and she's the one you're trying to get to take over your gardening chores. You already know to water deep when

you water. To figure out when it's time for another deep soaking, just step on your lawn. If the grass springs back from your footprint quickly, then things are okay. But if your footprint sticks around, leaving an impression in the grass, you had better do a rain dance or start up the sprinklers.

Most good-enough lawns can survive a dry summer with a once-a-week watering session. The secret is to run the sprinkler for at least two hours every time you water the lawn. Leave the sprinkler on all night long if that's what it takes to fully wet the top six inches of soil. Hard-packed clay soils have trouble absorbing water and sandy soils have trouble retaining water. Rich, loamy soil can go the longest between waterings. Another reason why improving your soil is the road to the luxury of laziness.

Treatment for Lawns with a Drinking Problem

The first step is to come clean and admit that your lawn has a problem. If you spend the summers quenching the never-ending thirst of your ungrateful lawn, watering two or three times a week just to keep it from turning brown, then join Overwaterers Anonymous. Take control of the problem now, or your lawn will always *be* a lush instead of *looking* lush. The fail-safe way to kick the habit is to improve your soil. The way to bolster your soil's water-storing talents is to add organic matter. Lots and lots of organic matter.

Rake in peat moss and relax on the watering.
Peat moss is almost as valuable as a comfy lounge chair to the lazy gardener. Organic matter like peat moss helps sandy soils to absorb more water and clay soils to drain better and move the moisture down to the grass roots. Organic matter comes in many forms: manure, straw, grass clippings — anything that adds bulk carbon to the soil. But peat moss has the most going for it. It's easy to work with, doesn't smell like a barnyard or harbor weed seeds, and it's sold almost everywhere, from hardware stores to supermarkets.

Getting peat moss into your soil before you seed a new lawn is easy. Just spread it two inches deep on top of the soil and till it into the top six inches of soil. Getting peat moss into your soil when a lawn is already growing is a bit more difficult. Follow these steps for lawn renovation if your old lawn has a drinking problem and the peat moss treatment is needed:

1. Aerate the problem lawn by removing plugs of soil. You can either hire out the job to a professional or rent the right power tools to do it yourself. If you have an older lawn that needs thatching, now's the time to do it. (See the thatching question on page 51.)

2. Rake up the thatch and soil plugs left lying on the grass after the above treatment.

3. Drag a bale of peat moss to the middle of the lawn. Cut it open and shovel out the contents, leaving little piles all over the lawn.

4. You may need to spray the lawn and peat moss with a fine mist of water to keep the piles from blowing away while you work.

5. Using the widest rake you can find, level the piles, so that the entire lawn gets a half-inch top dressing of peat moss. Try to work the peat moss down into the holes left by the aerating machine.

6. If water tends to sit on top of your soil, add sand mixed half-and-half with the peat moss.

7. If your soil is sandy and water runs right through it, mix packaged, weed-free steer manure with the peat moss.

You can repeat this treatment every spring until you have worked a large amount of peat moss into the soil.

Watering Worries Not to Worry About

■ Don't worry that watering at night will give your grass a disease. It rains at night, doesn't it? Set your sprinklers to come on in the wee hours of the morning. This is when you get the best water pressure. Early morning watering keeps your children and pets dry. It may even drown potential prowlers.

■ Don't worry that watering on a sunny day will scorch your grass. Pesticides and chemical fertilizers give lawns that scorched look, not watering on a hot day. Watering in the sun is not very efficient, however, since some of the moisture gets sapped up by the heat.

■ Don't worry that your brown-looking lawn is dead if watering restrictions during a drought are imposed. Most grass types will just go dormant during a time of water rationing and then spring back to life in the fall.

The Best Idea for the Lazy Lawn Perfectionist

The more perfect you want your lawn, the smaller your lawn should be. A tiny lawn can be hand-weeded and easily watered and fed. You can edge it, trim it, and mow it twice a week if you want, and still have time to live a leisurely life. If owning the perfect lawn is your goal in life, and you won't lower your standards, then shrink the square footage to compromise.

The Best Size for Any Lawn

Set your sprinkler in the middle of your lawn. Now turn it on high. The area that gets wet is all the grass you really need. If your sprinkler can't quite reach the corners of your lawn, then trust in fate. What can't be watered easily wasn't meant to be lawn. Replace those outer limits of lawn with drought-resistant groundcover plants or a gravel mulch instead.

Fertilizing without the Frenzy

Let's look at this fertilizing issue with an open mind. A lawn that is routinely fed with chemical fertilizers will, I admit, be one of the greenest lawns on the block. It will also be one of the most demanding. After a shot of lawn food, your grass will need to be mowed more often, watered more often, and thatched more often. (Don't worry if you don't know about thatch. I promise to explain it later.)

A lawn that is fed only once or maybe twice a year will still look pretty good, but it may slip into a summer dormant state and grow very slowly during the hot summer months. The promise of less lawn mowing during the heat of the summer is enough to boost the heart rate of any lazy gardener. A lawn allowed to go dormant in the summer does not have to look dead and ugly. Try adding water instead of chemical fertilizers to keep it on the green side.

So spend your summers in the lounge chair instead of lugging around sacks of fertilizer. Your flowers will be at their peak of beauty in the summer, so who's going to notice a less-than-perfect lawn? (Okay, lawn fanatics will notice, but not any sane people.)

Fertilizing the Memory of the Forgetful Gardener

Here are some memory tips that will remind you when to fertilize. This schedule is for northern gardeners only. Southern lawn growers should skip straight to "Fertilizing in the South," below.

September — Yellow school bus, yellow leaves, feed the lawn.
For the good-enough lawn, make your yearly application of lawn food in the fall. Fall feeding is best because the lawn is building up reserves for the winter in its root zone. A fall-fed lawn will green up sooner in the spring and get a chokehold on early season weeds.

March — St. Patrick's Day and daffodils, feed the lawn.
If you're willing to invest in a second feeding, then do it in early spring. Use a lawn

food with moss control if moss is moving in this month.

May — Mother's Day and lilacs in bloom, feed the lawn. This late spring feeding is for the lawn perfectionist. The best fertilizer to use at this time is an organic one like Lawn Restore, which will release nutrients slowly to the lawn. You can use a weed-and-feed product to wipe out the weeds at the same time you fertilize. Just try to wait until fall to fertilize again. Summer feedings can be hard on cool-season grasses that would rather lie dormant in the heat. Remember to try more water instead of more fertilizer to green up a browning summer lawn.

Fertilizing in the South

Northern grasses do not go dormant as early in the fall as southern grasses, and they generally green up much earlier in the spring. Southern grasses start to slow down when air temperatures reach about fifty degrees and go into dormancy with the first frost. In the spring, they stay dormant until temperatures climb above sixty degrees.

What all this means for the southern lawn grower is that lawns should be fertilized in the late spring and summer, rather than in the fall and early spring as in the North.

Lawn Fertilizers for the Lazy Gardener

Organic Fertilizers: Slow but Safe

The best lawn food is one that improves the soil while it greens up the lawn. If you pamper the soil instead of the lawn, you'll be on your way to healthy and more independent grass. Beef up your soil with organic lawn foods. These are bulkier, often smelly fertilizers that release nitrogen — the stuff that makes a lawn green — slowly into the soil. Organic lawn foods are long-term investments. You don't get the quick rush of green that traditional fertilizers provide with quick-release nitrogen, but over time a lawn fed with soil-improving organic fertilizers will demand less attention. Some cities sell sewage sludge to use as an organic lawn food. Blood meals and seed meals are other examples.

I am happy to report that conveniently packaged organic lawn fertilizers are now showing up in garden centers. One example is Lawn Restore made by the environmentally concerned Ringer Corporation. If you have poor soil and a lousy lawn, the road to restoration is the organic route. If you want your good-enough lawn to rival the perfectionist's patch of green, but without all the upkeep, then invest in organic lawn fertilizers. I will guarantee you a healthier lawn.

The Quick Fix

If you're not only lazy, but impatient as well, then hurry to the garden center and buy one of the new pre-mixed, pre-measured, ready-to-spray liquid lawn foods.

They come in plastic bottles that screw right onto your garden hose. You don't pour, measure, or add water. Just turn on the hose and the fertilizer solution mixes with the water as you walk slowly and aim the stuff at your lawn. You can even get these ready-to-spray solutions with weed killer or moss control mixed in. You can fertilize an average-sized lawn in less than ten minutes.

So what's the catch? The quick fix gives you almost instant green, but that all-important nitrogen doesn't stick around long in the soil. You also have to spray evenly to avoid streaks and take care not to overapply the product or you'll burn the lawn. Promise to read the label.

Still, the Quick Fix is great for using the week before your yard party or whenever you get a sudden urge for greener pastures.

Other Options

Buying bags of lawn food, lugging them home, and then loading up some kind of contraption to spread it on the lawn is an activity that seems an awful lot like hard work. Another option is to buy a liquid fertilizer, read all the fine print and measure out an exact amount in a hose-end spray bottle, add water to a certain mark and then carefully spray the lawn. All those steps with all those chances of messing up. Just another reason why fertilizing less often and using soil-improving organic fertilizers makes more sense. Lower your lawn standards, and you'll lower the stress in your life.

Tips for Fertilizing without Tragedy

■ Use a throw spreader instead of a drop spreader with granular lawn food. Throw spreaders come in both push and hand-held types, the latter with a little handle that you turn to distribute the fertilizer. Throw spreaders are more forgiving of your mistakes than other fertilizing systems, since the fertilizer is spread out in a less precise pattern. You also can cover more ground more quickly with a throw spreader, so you're done with the job and back relaxing on the couch is less time.

■ Fertilize the edges of your lawn first by walking around the perimeter. Then go back and forth across the lawn, being careful not to overlap when you get to the edge. Now you won't have to walk in the flower bed to turn around.

■ Read the instructions before you apply any fertilizer. Sit down in a comfortable chair with good light. Now read the directions twice and take notes if you need to. Why stand in a damp, dark garage and try to make sense from a bunch of fine print? Any job that can be done sitting down is something the lazy gardener shouldn't ignore.

■ If you're interrupted in the middle of fertilizing your lawn, just drop your hose, spreader, or other equipment right where you left off. Then, when you return to the job, you'll know exactly where to pick things up. You'll also be coaxed into finishing the job if you leave the equipment sitting outside.

Lime and the Lazy Gardener

Lime is cheap, it's easy to toss onto the lawn without any special equipment, and it is desperately needed by some soils. If your lawn doesn't green up after fertilizing, it may need lime.

You could go to the trouble of getting your soil tested, or you could just ask your neighbors with the lush lawn if they lime their soil every fall. In certain parts of the country, everybody has soil that is acid and needs to be sweetened up with lime. Areas that need lime are usually in climates where it rains a lot.

Buy dolomite limestone in the fall and sprinkle it all over the lawn, so the winter rains can wash it into the soil. An application of fifty pounds per 1,000 square feet is about right. If you can't find ground limestone for sale at any local garden centers, then conserve your energy. The soil in your area must not need it.

Weed Wars

Cutting through the confusion.
Forget the sprays, the spreaders, the chemicals and all the warnings printed on all those label instructions. There is a simple way to kill weeds. Just grab a screwdriver and dig out what you don't want in your lawn.

Before you groan and gripe at this humble suggestion, consider how much lawn you could weed in the time it takes to drive to a garden center, purchase a product, read about it, and then apply it to your lawn. Consider that some weed killer may drift onto your flowers. Consider the weather and wind conditions, which have to be just right for the chemical weed killers to work. Consider that you may be warned to stay off your lawn for twenty-four hours after using some weed-killing products. Why worry about such ominous-sounding warnings? Cut out the chemicals, and your children and pets can eat the lawn if they want. Cut out the weeds and you can eat a lot of them, too.

Once you commit yourself to hand-weeding, you'll probably lower your weed-free standards and become the healthy owner of a good-enough lawn. But, alas, the good-enough lawn is not good enough for you Lawn Fanatics, so let me sympathetically offer these tips for winning a few battles in the war of the weeds.

Don't waste money on weed-and-feed products until the weather warms up.
Read the label. Most weed-killing chemicals won't do their dirty work until the soil warms and weeds begin to grow. The late spring feeding around Mother's Day is the earliest you should use a weed-and-feed product in the North. If you're

concerned about chemicals that might drift onto your prized ornamentals, wait until late summer or early fall to use weed killers, or hire a professional to spray for you.

Spot-spray the weeds.
Don't drench your whole lawn in chemicals. Ready-to-use weed-killing products come pre-mixed in trigger-spray bottles. Lazy gardeners should always buy ready-to-use products. Otherwise you may buy a weed killer but never find the extra energy to play chemist and mix up a batch. It's more satisfying to shoot down each weed in hand-to-weed combat than to wage war using the "nuke it all" approach and dousing the entire lawn.

Smother the weeds with grass seeds.
Reseed your lawn each fall or spring to get a chokehold on some of the weeds. Just rake in a little peat moss or topsoil and sprinkle grass seed on top. Do this right before it rains. The thicker your lawn, the thinner the weed supply.

Mowing Matters — The Cutting Edge of Laziness

Cutting the lawn is no place to cut corners!
For once the lawn fanatics should be emulated. A neatly mowed and crisply edged lawn makes the whole yard look tidy. You can get away with more weeds and less green with a nicely cut lawn. Even the lazy gardener must mow the lawn regularly to keep it in "good-enough" shape.

Mow weekly, but mow it in minutes.
Grow yourself a smaller lawn. Don't grow it on a slope, under low-hanging tree branches or with any crazy corners. Only grow as much lawn as you can cut in a half hour. If you mow any more than that you may work up a sweat. Or miss your Saturday golf game, or ignore your prize begonias. Remember, there is life after lawn care, and lovely blooming things that also need your attention.

The Better Mowing Machine —
A Super Shocker for the Lazy Gardener

Return to the push mower.

Don't pass out. This radical, repulsive, and quite shocking idea makes sense if you just calm down enough to think about it. Here's my story.

Once upon a time, we had a medium-sized lawn on three different levels and a super-elite, lightweight mowing machine that rode on a cushion of air. I confess to owning a set of wimpy arm muscles, and lugging our old power mower up and down the stairs to mow all three levels was sinfully sweaty. Our new wonder machine was electric, so we didn't mess with gas but had to watch out for the long extension cord. To tell you the truth, I often pleaded pregnancy during those early years of marriage and avoided mowing the lawn. (If you're past the child-bearing years, opt for the osteoporosis excuse. Tell everyone your bones are thinning.)

In chapter two of this lawn story, we moved to a new home and put in a large lawn (5,000 square feet) on a level lot with two acres of gardens. We went hunting for the perfect power mower. My husband, the wanna-be lawn fanatic, voted for a gas-powered reel mower. A reel mower cuts using a whole set of blades with a clean scissorlike motion. This is why reel mowers give the neatest cut. These reel-type power mowers are the very same type that the professional turf-tenders use. They also come with a professional price tag. We were told that the old-fashioned push mower gives the same precision cut, since it, too, uses a reel of blades.

Enter the old-fashioned push mower. It was borrowed, actually, just for a couple of weeks to use on our newly seeded lawn. Heavy power mowers can damage tender new grasses. Those weeks turned into years, and that old push mower is still doing the job. Neatly, quickly, quietly, and at the right price.

We were silent at first about our discovery. Surely the rest of the world would cry that a return to a person-powered machine was a giant step backward for mankind. But then we noticed that others were beginning to leak news of the same discovery! A national gardening magazine (*Horticulture,* June 1988) featured an article called "Rediscovery of the Push Mower." A major department store started selling updated versions of this old-fangled machine. Mail-order garden supply catalogues even advertised modernized versions of this rummage-sale reject. Push mowers have been allowed back into proper society. Some say they never left. Here are ten reasons why every lazy gardener should consider spending some energy on a motorless mowing machine:

1. The reel-type cutting action of a push mower gives your lawn a cleaner cut. A neater trim means you can get away with a less-than-perfect lawn and still look like a lawn perfectionist.

2. You don't have to add gas, change spark plugs, or trip over an extension cord when you use a push mower.

3. A push mower is quiet and rhythmical. You can hear the birds singing in the trees, or the kids screaming as they fall out of them.

4. You can mow in the early morning hours and stay friends with your neighbors.

5. There won't be any gas fumes as you mow, or a lingering fuel scent on your fingers. You get to enjoy the scent of newly mowed grass.

6. It's cheap. Buy a push mower at a garage sale and go away for the weekend with the money you didn't spend on a power mower. Then sell your old power mower and go away for a longer weekend.

7. It's safe. You don't have to duck killer pebbles or window-seeking stones. I've asked my insurance agent to lower our homeowner premiums since we started the affair with our push mower. He thinks I'm kidding.

8. A push mower won't stall, cut out, or die — unless you do.

9. You can get out of mowing altogether. With a push mower, you can safely assign the lawn mowing to your older children. Too many teenagers lose fingers and toes mowing the family lawn with a power mower. Even mature adults suffer thousands of injuries every year operating power mowers. It's more difficult to earn a Purple Heart with a push mower.

10. Save time and money by getting rid of your health club membership. Cancel those aerobics classes and forego the expensive running shoes. Mowing a lawn with a push mower gives you the light aerobic workout you need. A push mower forces you to exercise at least weekly. Who needs a rowing machine when you have a mowing machine? Try to skip a weekly workout and you'll be punished with a lawn that's twice as hard to mow next time.

One final plug for the push mower. Technology has streamlined the heavy metal machine you remember sweating over as a kid. The new people-powered reel mowers are on the cutting edge of turf technology. Lazy gardeners may even learn to enjoy mowing the lawn.

How Close to Make the Cut

■ Avoid the short-cropped lawn. A lawn mowed very short belongs on a golf course, where they plant a special type of grass that can tolerate the torture. Most northern lawns contain some Kentucky bluegrass, and bluegrass hates to be mowed any shorter than one-and-a-half inches.

■ You can adjust the mower blades for an even higher cut in the summer, so the longer grass can shade the soil. When the soil is shaded, your lawn requires less water.

■ For a good-enough lawn in the North, just set the blades so they'll cut at one-and-a-half inches all year long.

■ To measure how high your mower cuts, set it on cement. Now use a ruler to measure the distance from the ground to the cutting blade.

■ Southern lawns can be cut closer. If you live where the snow never falls, then your lawn mix may include a lot of warm-season grasses like Bermuda, or even Dichondra, which is not technically a grass at all, but a tropical perennial herb. These lawns can be mowed very short. Set your mower height at one-half inch all year long. St. Augustine, centipede, and zoysia grasses should all be cut higher, though — more like northern lawns.

■ If you're trying to grow grass in a shady area, leave it two or even three inches long. It needs that extra leaf area to absorb the tiny bit of solar energy that comes its way.

If You Have a Gigantic Lawn to Mow

■ Forget about the push mower until you scale down that lawn.

■ Invest in a riding mower.

■ Pay a lawn service or neighborhood kid to mow it for you.

■ Use a power mower that covers the widest section of lawn in one sweep.

■ Barter out the job to someone who enjoys mowing. (I know a widow who bakes a pie every Saturday for the gentleman across the street who mows her lawn. I keep waiting for something else to start growing between the two of them.)

Capitalize on the Clippings — To Collect or Not to Collect

■ Leave the clippings right where they are if you have a large lawn or use a riding mower. They will dry up and slip into the soil, returning about a third of their nitrogen to the lawn.

■ Collect the clippings if you're a lawn fanatic or if your lawn is small. You get a tidier look, and the grass clippings will come in handy. The lazy way is to use a bag that attaches right to your mowing machine. Empty the bag into a wheelbarrow that you've parked nearby.

■ Always collect the clippings if you mow during cool, rainy weather. Fungal disease moves in when wet globs of matted grass lie around. In shady areas, these matted grass clippings will encourage moss. When grass clippings congregate in clumps, get out the rake and start collecting.

■ Have a designated dumping spot that's easy to get to. Hide it behind a bush or low fence.

■ Grass clippings can be composted by layering them with leaves and soil. Spread a tarp on top to keep away the flies.

■ You can dump grass clippings in a wild section of the yard to smother the weeds.

■ If you have the room, spread your clippings all around your trees, shrubs, and flowers. Use a very thin layer, so the cut grass can dry out before it has a chance to mat down.

■ Dried grass clippings work well as a weed-blocking mulch. More about mulching in Chapter Nine.

■ If you have extra-long grass to cut, the clippings will fill up your bag quickly. Divide the job into two jobs instead. Mow one day and let the long clippings lie in the sun. Rake the next day, and the clippings will be lighter and easier to handle.

A Picture-Perfect Border to Frame the Lawn

Get control with a border.
Use railroad ties, landscaping timbers, bricks, 2 by 4s, bender boards, or rigid plastic edging. Anything to define your spreading lawn and keep it from taking over the flower beds. A border will give a good-enough lawn that crisp clean look that the fanatics are after. (See illustration below.)

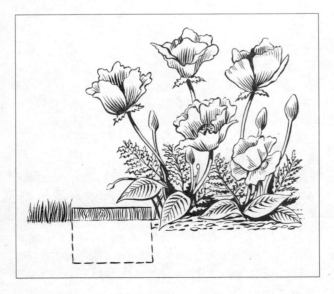

Peel away the work with a mowing strip. Any lawn-level strip that you can use to balance one wheel of your lawn mower on can be used to cut close to the edge of the lawn and eliminate hand-edging. Put in a border slightly higher than the level of your lawn and it can serve as a mowing strip as well as a lawn border. (See illustration on next page.)

Tie up loose ends with a string trimmer.

The handy string trimmer cuts down grass and weeds with a nylon string. The best known string-trimmer is the Weed Eater brand. Just run a string-trimmer around the edge of your lawn every other week. This will keep the grass low around any raised borders. If you use a string-trimmer, you won't have to put in a mowing strip level with the ground.

Hide the edge under cover.

Use a groundcover or sprawling plants around the edge of your lawn. This won't give you a crisp, clean edge, but it will keep down the grass that your lawn mower can't reach. Don't worry if the groundcover starts to take over the area you set aside for a lawn. Remember our Golden Rule and stop arguing with Mother Nature. You don't really need all that lawn, anyway.

Plans for Shrinking the Size of Your Lawn

Stop just wishing your lawn would go away. Put into action a plan to make it disappear.

1. Put in a circular driveway.

2. Plant groundcovers along the borders and let them spread.

3. Add paths, courtyards, or patios.

Most-Asked Lawn Care Questions

Q. *Help! My lawn is being taken over by an invasion of moss. At certain times of the year I have more moss than lawn. What can I do to get my lawn back?*
A. The invasion of the moss monster occurs when you try to grow lawn in a place that is too shady, too wet, or on very poor soil. Use a lawn food with moss control in early spring. If the moss is really hanging heavy, you'll have to use a liquid moss killer. Murdered moss is not a pretty sight. It turns brown and black. Rake out the dead moss, spread a thin layer of topsoil, and scatter grass seed throughout the area. Sprinkle lime on your lawn each fall. Moss hates lime. Aerate a wet lawn and

rake in some sand. Let in more light by pruning the lower branches of your trees. Fertilize your lawn more often. If the moss marches back after all this effort, then give up. Encourage the moss and kill off the lawn. Add a few giant rocks and a stone pagoda. Call it a Japanese moss garden and meditate away your desire for a lawn.

Q. *We have mushrooms popping up in our lawn. What can I use to kill them?*
A. Give those uninvited fungi a swift kick in the cap to keep them from spreading. Clean up the fallen mushrooms to keep the curious from tasting them. There are no sprays or magic formulas to keep mushrooms out of the lawn. You might want to dig down to the root of the problem and see what is rotting below your lawn that is encouraging the mushrooms. One homeowner found a leather shoe buried beneath a persistent patch of mushrooms.

Q. *We just moved to a new house and took possession of a lawn that is in terrible shape. There are more weeds than grass. The soil is hard and the lawn is bumpy. Should we try to improve this dismal lawn or kill it off and start all over again?*
A. It's always easier to renovate an old lawn than to start a new one from scratch. It just takes a lot longer. If you've got more time than money and more patience than energy, make the most out of what you've got by doing one thing to improve it each season.

Spring: Aerate and thatch the old lawn by renting the proper tools or by hiring the job out to a professional lawn company. Spread a one-inch layer of topsoil or peat moss on top of the lawn and work this organic matter into the aeration holes with a rake. Sprinkle new seed on top.

Summer: Work on the weeds. Use a spot weed killer for maximum coverage or dig them out by hand all summer long.

Fall: Now is the time to reseed with the top-of-the-line seed mix. Sprinkle peat moss or topsoil into the old lawn and sprinkle the new seed evenly over the surface. Keep the lawn moist until the new seed is established.

Late Fall: There's still time to fertilize with an organic fall and winter lawn food. Add lime if the soil in your area is acid.

Q. *Our neighbor has a dog that does his business on my lawn each day. What can I do about the dead spots this leaves?*
A. Doggy burns are similar to fertilizer burns — both are caused by an overdose of nitrogen. Drown the area with water immediately after the deposit is made. This will wash part of the poison away from the tender grass roots. If the burn is concentrated in an obvious spot, go cut yourself a piece of sod from a discreet corner (your neighbor's lawn, perhaps?) and fit this new sod into the bare spot. There are animal repellent sprays that work on most dogs. The trick is to be persistent and assertive for at least ten days, until the offending animal becomes ingrained with new habits. You could always invest in a fence, or a very thorny hedge.

Q. *What is the easiest way to get rid of moles or gophers? The little earth mounds they leave are ruining my lawn.*
A. The easiest way is to hire someone to trap the varmints. It takes skill to set and bait a proper trap. Professional trappers can be found under exterminators in the yellow pages of the phone book. Pay by the pelt. If the trap does not produce a culprit, you don't have to produce a payment. Gassing, poison, and wind toys may scare off moles and gophers for awhile, but they often return to haunt your yard again.

Q. *What is thatch?*
A. Thatch is a buildup of grass stems and roots that sit on the surface of the soil down in between the grass blades. If thatch is allowed to get too thick, it can block water and fertilizer from getting to the grass roots. The easiest way to get rid of thatch is to rent a power thatching rake whenever you need it. You can tell if thatch is a problem when water doesn't penetrate quickly on a dry lawn or if your lawn feels spongy or padded when you walk on it. The best time to thatch is in the spring or early fall. Some lawns build thatch rapidly — many of the warm-season grasses have this problem and need thatching once a year. Other lawns with a lot of ryegrass in them may never need thatching. Thatch your lawn at least once in its lifetime. See if it improves it enough to make thatching it again worthwhile.

Q. *My lawn is dying in spots. It turns yellow first and then slowly starts to die out.*
A. Dig up a large chunk of the yellowing turf, roots and all. Put the specimen in a plastic bag and immediately present it to your nearest lawn detective. The lawn experts in most neighborhoods are as close as the nearest garden center. The place that sells grass seed and lawn fertilizers is usually a better bet than the nursery that specializes in blooming plants. If the manager doesn't know the answer to your problem, he'll know how to find out. Lawn insects and diseases vary greatly across the country. Trust local experts to be your lawn doctors. They get very familiar with the current diseases or insects making the rounds in your area.

※ CHAPTER THREE

Flowering Shrubs: The Backbone of Carefree Color

Imagine a yard with flowers blooming from early spring to early winter. Don't picture neat little rows of knee-high marigolds or ground-covering petunias. Think of a garden with masses of flowers blooming at eye level. Flowers that don't need staking, fertilizing, or watering and, most important of all, flowers that won't be eaten by slugs and bugs. Now imagine that these flowers need to be planted only once to bloom again year after year. Sound like the Garden of Eden? Any garden can become as carefree and colorful as Paradise if the blooms and the beauty come from hardy flowering shrubs.

Ten Beautiful Bonuses of Blooming Bushes

1. You can choose from a wide variety of blooming times, colors, and flower forms. Plan a border using ten or twelve different shrubs and you can arrange to have something in bloom almost year-round.

2. Shrubs have woody, stiff branches that hold the flowers up closer to eye and nose level. These blooms never need to be staked or supported like some tall flowering plants.

3. When a shrub blooms, you get hundreds, often thousands, of blossoms. A gigantic floral display, full-blown in full bloom. Not your shrinking-violet or plain-as-a-daisy dab of color. You can steal blooming branches for indoor use and still not make a dent in the outdoor display. Compare this to the small handful of flowers that result when you plant a single bulb or seed.

4. Shrubs live longer and require less care than perennial flowers or bedding plants. Plant a shrub once, and enjoy it for a lifetime.

5. Flowering shrubs often have large and efficient root systems. This gives them a survival edge. They rarely need extra water and will thrive in many different types of soil and weather conditions. There's no need to fuss with fertilizers year after year, either. Some shrubs even grow weak and faded if you try to force-feed them with plant food.

6. Hardy blooming shrubs are hard to kill. They are tough enough to take cold winds, long winters, and early frosts. The deciduous shrubs that stand naked all winter without their leaves are actually the best-equipped to handle the cold. They slip into dormancy and sleep right through the nasty weather. Lilacs are famous for this. Other shrubs that adapt easily to hot, dry summers in milder climates are escallonia, potentilla, and the yuccas.

7. Insects and diseases ignore most hardy shrubs. These plant enemies much prefer to attack the soft and succulent growth of tender annual flowers and perennials.

8. Shrubs take up a lot of room. This is important to the lazy gardener who wants a very small lawn. You can fill up the yard with inexpensive, fast-growing shrubs until there's no room left for a demanding lawn.

9. Blooming shrubs, especially those that have winter berries, attract the birds. Every good gardener enjoys the benefits of bug-eating birds, and every lazy gardener depends on the free pest-control service that the birds provide.

10. Flowering shrubs can be used to solve landscape problems. They can hold the soil on a steep hillside, screen an ugly view, block the wind, and define your garden boundaries. All this and flowers, too.

How to Pick the Winners — Finding the Best Bloomers for You.

■ Stick your nose into your neighbors' shrubbery. Notice what shrubs are in bloom and doing nicely as you drive around town. Parks and arboretums will be a big help in guiding you to the blooming shrubs that do best in your climate.

■ Look at what's still alive and blooming in the older part of town: the shrubs that blossom around rental complexes, the overgrown shrubs that surround rundown homes, and those that bloom proudly amidst the rubble of vacant lots. These are the survivors that will bloom through benign neglect.

■ Choose the old-fashioned flowering shrubs that were grown in your grandparents' garden. Hydrangea, lilac, mock orange, and bridal veil have been blooming for generations, and one reason they're becoming popular again is because they're so tough.

■ You can usually get proper identification of any blooming shrub by taking a piece of a branch to your local nursery. If the nursery people don't recognize the plant, they'll know where you can go for proper I.D.

■ When you do find a blooming shrub for sale, don't be coerced into adopting it right away. Realize that those gorgeous blooms will only adorn the shrub for about one month out of twelve. Find out what the shrub looks like the rest of the year.

This reminds me of a forsythia story. Forsythia is a shrub that blooms very early in the spring. Its brilliant yellow blooms are displayed on graceful and gracious-looking branches. So lovely is the forsythia in bloom that one home-owner (Let's call him Mr. Gold) planted this shrub right up close to his front door. In two years' time, the gracefully arching branches had overtaken the front porch and had to be chopped off at midarch by midsummer. The shrub was soon sprawling all over the porch again and began taking over the steps as well. Another pruning in late summer removed the flower buds and prevented Mr. Gold's forsythia from blooming the following spring.

This cycle of severe summer butchering and then a no-show at bloom time was repeated year after year. Mr. Gold had himself a forsythia that never bloomed, that was unattractive all summer, fall, and winter, and that continually tried to capture the tiny front porch and force its way into his home through the windows. He wondered why he had ever paid money for such a nuisance shrub.

This story is not supposed to steer you away from the forsythia. It is, in fact, a perfect shrub for the lazy gardener. But any time a shrub grows large and sprawling, or has rather plain foliage when not in bloom, it needs to be grown away from the house where it has room to arch out and can be enjoyed from a distance. A forsythia shrub aglow with golden blooms on an early spring day is a glorious sight. It's just not a shrub that looks happy when confined to a small area.

Many flowering shrubs look rather plain when not in bloom. The lesson here is to check out the habits of any shrub before investing in it. If you need color in a small area, then buy a shrub that stays small or grows very slowly. Mr. Gold tried to keep his forsythia small with frequent pruning. Mother Nature responded by withholding the spring blossoms. He had never heard the lazy gardening oath: Don't fight Mother Nature.

(Just in case you're wondering, Mr. Gold eventually gave up and trans-planted that forsythia to another spot. He stopped chopping it up and now reports beautiful blooms every spring and ignores the plant the rest of the year. He grows roses next to his front porch.)

Putting Flowering Shrubs to Work

The lazier you are, the more shrubs you need!

If you're too lazy to build and maintain a fence:
Plant a solid line of shrubbery. Camellia, rhododendrons, and photinia grow fast and make a colorful barrier in cool, moist climates. Try holly, barberry, and

cotoneaster in colder parts of the country.

If you're too lazy to plant bulbs each fall for spring flowers:
Put in a forsythia or flowering quince bush. You'll enjoy early spring blooms and have branches to prune and use indoors. Unlike bulbs, rodents and slugs won't bother these early spring shrubs, and you only have to plant them once.

If you're too lazy to water during dry spells:
Put in a collection of drought-resistant bloomers. Potentilla, cotoneaster, and buddleia or butterfly bush will survive in dry and sunny spots even if you forget to water.

If you're too lazy to spray air freshener:
Scent your yard with the blooms from lilac, mock orange, and lavender, then open a window to bring the freshness indoors. If you have an outside clothesline, plant a fragrant shrub nearby and you'll be sleeping on scented sheets.

If you're too lazy to trim a hedge:
Plant a row of compact shrubbery that keeps its tidiness without ever needing a haircut. Japanese holly, Hino crimson azaleas, and dwarf barberry are low-growing shrubs that stay neat and tidy.

If you're too lazy to feed the birds:
Provide a bird buffet every winter with shrubs that bear berries. Cotoneaster and pyracantha will provide food for the birds even if you forget. Lazy gardeners really need birds. They act as hired assassins for the bugs breaking into your yard.

If you're too lazy to drain off the wet spots in your yard:
Just fill in the spot with winterberry, pussy willow, and redtwig (also called "red osier") dogwood shrubs. Underplant the shrubs with a moisture-loving groundcover and you'll never have to look at standing water again.

If you're too lazy to rake leaves in the fall:
Plant a smoke tree or burning bush for fantastic fall color that won't smother the grass with falling leaves. You can enjoy maximum fall color with shrubs and still have time to watch football games on the weekend.

Too lazy to landscape at your seaside vacation home:
Plant Scotch broom and bearberry all over the property. You'll have no-fuss blooms at windy ocean sites.

Too lazy to put in annual flowers (bedding plants) for summer color:
Plant summer-blooming shrubs up close to your patio. Dwarf buddleia, potentilla,

and hydrangea are compact enough plants to grow near the house or next to a deck or patio. Nobody will even notice the missing marigolds.

Too lazy to plant flowers in your window boxes and patio pots each year:
Pot up a camellia, a dwarf rhododendron, or a heavenly bamboo in that wooden whiskey barrel. Keep potted shrubs close to the house for winter protection and remember to keep them watered and fertilized. The roots of potted shrubs can't spread out and take care of themselves, so they need more attention than a shrub in the ground.

Too lazy to store your fuchsia basket every winter, and too cheap to buy a new one every spring:
Plant a hardy Magellan fuchsia this year in a protected spot. All you have to do is remember to prune the top growth to the ground each fall, and your fuchsia will return each spring and bloom all summer. This fuchsia shrub will survive in cold winter areas.

Too lazy to cut down the shade trees that took over your landscape and drowned you in darkness:
Grow shade-loving sweet box *(Sarcococca ruscifolia)* and enjoy fragrant flowers in very early spring. This evergreen shrub survives in the very darkest of shade as long as you add plenty of peat moss to the soil and remember to water before it gets dry. Perfect for that dark area on the north side of the house. There's also a whole family of rhododendrons, camellias, and azaleas that tolerate the shade in mild winter areas. Redtwig (red osier) dogwood thrives in shade and wet soil in the coldest of climates.

Too lazy to terrace a steep slope:
Groundcovers do a quick job, but for added height and color you can add heather, forsythia, and Scotch broom to fill in on hillsides. Not only will these shrubs add color, but they have penetrating root systems that help stabilize the hillsides.

Watering Tips for Lazy Shrub Growers

Most shrubs need no extra irrigation once they get used to your yard. That first summer can be tough, however, so make sure you help out with extra water during the formative first year.

■ Water slowly with a dripping hose. Leave the hose running ever so gently next to the roots of the shrub. A deep soaking will take hours, but then you won't have to worry about watering again for weeks.

■ Plant your shrubs near the border of your lawn and then turn up the sprinkler high enough so that it reaches the shrub roots each time you water the lawn.

■ Save your old leaky hose or purchase a length of hose that already leaks. Lay this hose along the feet of your shrub border and then just hook up the hose when you need it. Cover the perforated hose with bark or another mulch if you want to hide your watering shortcut.

Fertilizing Beautiful Bloomers

There's no need to get fancy here. You can forget about fertilizing if you really want to. Most shrubs do just fine on their own. Any shrub that demands constant attention and special fertilizers shouldn't be growing in your yard. Sometimes problems crop up, and there are stubborn lilacs and rhododendrons that can be coaxed into bloom with a well-planned shot of plant food. If you get the urge to fertilize and don't mind pampering your plants a bit, remember these tips when feeding shrubs:

■ Spread gritty or granular plant foods around the drip line of the shrub. This is the place where water drips off of the outermost branches and leaves. Use a hose to water in the plant food as soon as you fertilize.

■ Spread dead flowers, grass clippings, and a top layer of soil or bark mulch around the base of your shrubs to keep out the weeds. This mini compost pile will trickle down all the nutrients your shrubs should need.

■ Shrubs like mock orange and lilac that like the soil a bit alkaline will smile if you remember to throw a handful of lime at their feet each fall. If you don't have any dolomite lime handy, you can substitute wood ashes. That way you can clean out the fireplace and feed the shrubbery at the same time. Rhododendrons and azaleas like acid soil. Keep the lime away from them.

■ You can spray liquid plant food right on the foliage of your shrubs. Certain acid-loving plants such as rhododendrons and azaleas suffer from *chlorosis*, or lack of iron, when the soil is not kept acid enough. This condition turns their leaves a mottled yellow. It also gives me an excuse to branch off into a shrubby success story.

I am sometimes called upon to make yard calls to visit sickly plants. My favorite patients are the pale yellow and sickly looking rhododendrons, azaleas, and camellias. Nine times out of ten I can perform a plant-healing miracle just by prescribing a dose of iron sulphate or iron chelate for these pale-faced plants. The results are especially impressive if the iron is sprayed onto the leaves of the plant. Iron is absorbed quickly, and a rhodie can go from ugly to unbelievably green in less than a week. Liquid chelated iron is sold at large garden centers. A word of caution here: Yellow leaves are a symptom of many different problems, and the iron treatment will only work if the yellow leaves are due to iron-poor soil.

Pruning for More Blooming

If you have no urge to control the size of your shrubs and they bloom well enough for you, then put away those pruning shears and relax. Most flowering shrubs survive splendidly with very little touch-ups with the pruning shears. You can do some good with some polite pruning, and prolific blooms are often the result.

Don't prune a flowering shrub more than once a year. Flowers take a long time to form, and you'll be aborting little flower buds if you trim your blooming shrubs every two or three months. You'll also ruin your reputation as a lazy gardener.

Forget the poodle-balling, lollipop shapes and boxy rectangles. Have you ever seen plants in the wild grow in such silly shapes? Mother Nature never intended her plants to grow in geometric forms. Allow the graceful, spreading natural shape of the shrub to predominate. There's a reason why free-growing shrubs stay healthier and live longer then their mutilated and restrained brethren. Good air circulation keeps down the bugs and disease. Dense and squatty shrubs don't enjoy the benefits of free-flowing air. They have dark, dank interiors that are the favorite hangouts of dangerous characters of the gardening underworld.

Prune out old dead wood and encourage vigorous new shoots. I know this is a lot easier said than done. Lazy gardeners will have to bend down low and get underneath the shrub and then decide what is an old branch and what is a new one. Spending time on your hands and knees getting dirty is not the kind of sport lazy gardeners go in for. Be grateful that most of these shrubs don't need thinning too often. Follow these tips to get you through the pruning period as painlessly as possible:

■ Spread your tarp under the shrub before you begin the operation. This will give you someplace clean to kneel and also catch the pruning crumbs that fall to the ground for no-fuss cleanup.

■ Use very sharp shears and store them indoors, not in a cold and damp shed. Rusty shears take too much energy to operate.

■ Look for thick stems emerging from the center of the shrub. Remove a third of the thickest branches, cutting as close to the ground as possible. This will encourage fresh side shoots to pop up with more energy.

■ Be ruthless with any dead, damaged, or diseased branches. Follow them right to the trunk or ground and amputate.

■ Clean up any small, weak shoots that are growing toward the center of the shrub. Toss them onto the tarp along with dead leaves and other trapped debris. Hands off any bird nests you happen to find in the center of the bush.

■ Now stand back and admire your work. If you still see a few wayward branches that reach out farther than the rest or lie like untidy arms on the ground, go ahead and trim them back to a third of their original selves.

The Necessary Massacre

Sometimes a neglected shrub just gets out of control. It may be so old that the lower half of the shrub is bare of foliage, or so tall that the flowers are out of reach. The untamed form may look too wild and the shrub too thick and tangled with an overpopulation of branches. This type of situation calls for drastic action. Some shrubs respond better than others to the treatment. Some shrubs never recover from the shock and die of embarrassment. We're talking about drastic pruning. Drastic as in cutting the shrub right off at its ankles, leaving nothing but a few inches of stump.

I admit to resorting to this grisly form of massacre when nothing else seems to work. When the only alternative is ripping the thing out by its roots. I'm always surprised at how often the drastic pruning job produces fantastic results. Lilacs cut to the ground sprout up full and compact and bloom again in two or three years. Tall and rangy rhododendrons emerge the next spring, flush with new growth budding out from the hideous stumps. Before you attempt a necessary massacre, be advised that this is risky surgery. It takes several years for full recovery.

When to Prune Your Flowering Shrubs

■ If it blooms in the winter or spring, prune it soon after the flowers fade, or, if you need cut flowers, go ahead and trim it up when it's blooming.

■ If it blooms in the summer of fall, prune in early spring. Then the shrub will have plenty of time to form new buds before bloom time.

Homecoming Hints for Easier Transplanting

When you go to a nursery to buy a shrub, they come either potted up, balled and burlapped, or bareroot. A potted shrub is simply sold growing in its own container. A balled and burlapped shrub has been dug from the ground, and its round root ball is wrapped in burlap and tied in place with twine. Bareroot shrubs are sold in early spring before the leaves have started to unfold. The roots are bare of any soil, but are often packed inside a plastic bag and surrounded with moist sawdust.

■ The easiest and cheapest way to buy a shrub or tree is bareroot. Without the soil around the roots, your new shrub will be lightweight and easy to transport home. The lazy gardener appreciates any plant that can be picked up with one hand. Unfortunately bareroot plants must be planted while still dormant, so this means tramping outdoors during cold weather and digging a hole for the bare and leafless twig you just purchased bareroot. Not very exciting work.

■ Shrubs with compact root balls that are wrapped in burlap are a bit heavier to lift, but they can still be set on their sides for the ride home, and you can plant them later on in the growing season. This means you can add a flowering azalea shrub to your yard on a warm spring day, while it's in glorious bloom. It's easy to get the balled and burlapped plant positioned properly in the new hole you dig because the root ball is wrapped up and easy to shift around. Don't worry about removing the burlap. Just untie the twine and fill in around the burlapped ball with soil.

■ Potted shrubs can be moved to your yard at any time of year. The biggest hassle is prying the plant from its clinging pot. Never grab the shrub by the neck and try to lift it out of the pot. Instead, turn the whole works upside down and bang the rim of the pot on the edge of your wheelbarrow. This little maneuver catches the stubborn pot off guard, and the plant can slip easily out of its prison.

■ Shrubs need to be planted at the same depth or soil level that they were growing at before. Use the long handle of your shovel as a level to lay across the hole once you get the plant positioned. This way it will be easy to tell if you've got the root ball higher or lower then the ground level around it.

■ Remember to ask at the nursery about the mature size of your new shrub. If you don't have an expert handy to ask, look up the shrub's size in a gardening encyclopedia. The mature size of any shrub is very important to a lazy gardener. Overambitious shrubbery is a lot of work. Remember Mr. Gold and his fast-acting forsythia.

■ Fill in with groundcover plants and annual flowers while you wait for your young shrubs to grow and mature. A border of newly planted shrubs won't look like much at first.

■ Form a collar or ridge of soil several inches high around the shrub immediately after you plant it. Now fill the basin with water; that way, you won't waste precious moisture because of surface runoff. You can use rocks or blocks of wood if your soil is too sandy to mold into a water-holding basin.

■ Don't try growing any plants under the eaves of the house where the rain never hits. You don't want the hassle of hand-watering do you? The soil right up close to the house may be tainted with lime if you have a new cement foundation. Acid-loving plants hate lime.

■ Avoid positioning a shrub in the drip line directly under the edge of your roof.

Gutters have a tendency to clog up during heavy rains. The water comes rushing down off the slope of your roof and smashes into any plants in its path. These little disasters usually occur when the shrub is in beautiful bloom.

■ Dig the holes for your new shrubs first, before you even go out and purchase them. This way you'll be sure to get the shrubs planted as soon as possible. Lazy gardeners sometimes let new plants sit around for weeks while they work up the energy needed to dig a hole. Shame on us.

My Top Twelve Shrubs for Year-Round Color	
FORSYTHIA	BUDDLEIA
RHODODENDRON	SMOKE TREE
HYDRANGEA	LILAC
ROSE OF SHARON	MOCK ORANGE
QUINCE	SPIRAEA
VIBURNUM	COTONEASTER

■ When you take out that first shovelful of topsoil from the planting hole, set it apart from the rest of the lighter colored soil below. When you are ready to add the new shrub, that darker topsoil should go in first, so it's closest to the hungry roots of the new transplant.

■ Add peat moss to the planting hole if your soil is very sandy or hard-packed with clay. Very hot water will moisten peat moss in a hurry. (Dry peat moss is difficult to mix into the soil.) You can also substitute compost or oldy-moldy manure for the peat moss.

Forcing the Issue

One of the special joys of spring-blooming shrubs is that they can be pruned in the dead of winter and the bare branches brought indoors. The warmth of your home will force the flower buds to open early, while the mother shrub outdoors sleeps on through the winter.

Pussy willows, forsythia, quince, and kerria have blossoms that are easy to force indoors. Don't go to all the bother of soaking cut branches in a bathtub or keeping them in a dark closet. These are both suggestions that come from flower fanatics — I love flowers, but I'm not about to share my bathtub with them. You can simplify the forcing process with this one-step method:

Gather up one section of the newspaper and head outside on a mild winter day. But don't get too anxious. Branches can be forced into bloom just six weeks to one month earlier than Mother Nature's original timetable. In areas with lots of freezing weather, forcing may be done in March; in milder climates, try it in February.

Lay your newspaper right on the wet ground beneath the shrub you want to steal flowers from. Now thin the plant by cutting out the inner branches. These are the whips or sticks you will use for forcing. Lay the cut branches on top of the moist newspaper as you cut. When you've got a bundle, wrap the newspaper around the top half of the branches, secure with a rubber band, and just plunk the bottom half of the bundle into a vase of warm water. Set these wrapped branches in a cold room for a couple of weeks, checking periodically until you see signs of life. When the buds break, unveil the arrangement and place it near a bright window. You'll have lovely winter blooms without giving up either tub or closet space.

Most-Asked Questions About Flowering Shrubs

Q. *I bought a hydrangea bush when it was in bloom, and the flowers were pink. Several years have passed, and now the flowers are blue. How can I get back my pink hydrangea blossoms?*
A. Hydrangeas definitely have a problem with gender identity. In acid soil, they bloom a bold and masculine blue, but put the same plant in a more alkaline soil and it takes on feminine traits and turns pink. If you really need to have a pink bloomer, then sprinkle dolomite lime around the roots of the plant this fall. Use one shovelful of lime for a four-foot-tall hydrangea shrub. Lime makes the soil more alkaline, and so the blossoms will start to turn pink again. It may take several years of the lime treatment before your hydrangea gives up its preferred gender and turns pretty in pink. At least your blue hydrangea has taught you something about your soil. Now you know that you garden with soil that is naturally acid. You should choose plants like azaleas, rhododendrons, and blue hydrangeas that like what you've got.

Q. *We planted a lilac shrub five years ago and it still hasn't bloomed. The leaves look nice and green and the shrub is now over five feet tall. How can we get this lazy plant to give us some lilacs?*
A. Before you place all the blame on the lilac, make sure you've planted it where it gets afternoon sun and that it gets water during summer droughts. Now get tough and use a sharp shovel to cut into the root zone of the stingy lilac. Cutting the roots like this will also make slits in the ground so you can sprinkle in some superphosphate fertilizer. Superphosphate is the stuff orchardists sometimes use to force fruit trees into bloom. It is sold at large garden centers or feed and farm-supply outlets. You can also add some dolomite lime or wood ashes to the soil along with the fertilizer. Pamper the lilac with extra water all summer long, and if you aren't rewarded with fragrant blooms by the second spring, ruthlessly rip it out. Any plant that won't put out after you've fussed and pampered it along doesn't deserve to grow in the yard of a lazy gardener.

Q. *My neighbor and I each have a forsythia bush. His blooms early every spring, but the flowers are not as yellow as mine. When my forsythia does bloom, the color is brilliant yellow, but sometimes only half the buds will open. Does the guy next door just* *have a greener thumb, or what?*

A. The words "new and improved" are often used with good reason in the plant world. There are several species and many varieties of forsythia, and this is true for other flowering shrubs as well. Your neighbor must have a hardier variety of forsythia that blooms reliably because it doesn't get freaked out by an extra-cold winter. Your forsythia was bred for fancier yellow flowers, but you pay for the frills with a plant that isn't as cold-hardy. Move your forsythia to a more protected location or find out what variety your neighbor has. It's probably *Forsythia ovata* or "Korean forsythia," a very cold-hardy plant and a good choice for the lazy gardener. If you want low-maintenance shrubs for your yard, then go for the "new and improved" varieties that promise hardiness, disease resistance, or compact growth habits. Fancy colors and flower shapes rank second in priority.

Q. *We have a beautiful blooming shrub that gets covered with fragrant white flowers every June. We found out that this lovely plant is called a "mock orange," and so we bought several more plants from a reputable mail-order nursery and planted them in the same area as our giant mock orange. This is the second spring, and those new plants still haven't bloomed. Should we write to the company for a refund?*

A. Lazy gardeners must also be very patient gardeners. It usually takes two or three years for very young shrubs to grow to blooming size. If your baby mock orange plants have made new growth and appear healthy enough, then stop your fretting and let them enjoy a carefree childhood before you expect the same performance that your mature shrub gives. You can thin out a few of the inner branches of your old mock orange to encourage more blooms, but the young plants shouldn't need trimming. Concentrate on giving the young shrubs plenty of water and a bit of fertilizer, and keep the area around them free of weeds and grasses.

Q. *We have some huge flowering shrubs called spiraea. They need to be severely pruned because we are adding on to our house and they take up too much room. When is the best time to cut these plants right down to the ground?*

A. You can perform this type of major surgery in late winter. This way, the patient will be under the anesthetic of winter dormancy and won't suffer as much shock. Don't expect instant recovery when you massacre an overgrown shrub. You may have to wait a year or two before the plant feels up to flowering again. Spiraeas are also quite adaptable if you need to prune them at other times of the year.

Q. *My mother has offered to share some of the flowering shrubs in her yard. I would like a start of her rhododendrons and a few other blooming plants. Can I just use a shovel to split the roots apart and take home a section of her shrubs?*

A. Stop right now before you ruin your mother's garden! Many flowering shrubs such as rhododendrons have compact root systems, and you can't just barge in with a shovel and start splitting things apart. There are all sorts of ways to share shrubs by taking cuttings, rooting them in sand, etc., but the easiest way for the lazy gardener to propagate shrubs is by surface layering. What you do is bend a branch to the ground, make a cut halfway through the branch, and then bury the injured section in the soil. Use a brick or bent coat hanger to keep the branch in place until roots form at the site of the injury. In a year or so, sever the new plant from its mother and you have yourself a new plant without the hassles of getting it started in a greenhouse. The bad news is that not all shrubs will cooperate and root by surface layering. Still, it doesn't take much energy to try. (See illustrations.)

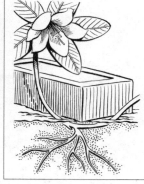

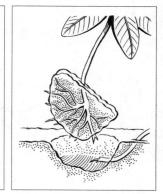

To propagate a shrub by surface layering, make a cut halfway through a branch and bury it.

Hold the branch in place until roots begin to form at the cut.

In a year or so, sever the new growth from the mother and transplant.

Q. *Should I rake maple leaves around my flowering shrubs for winter protection?*
A. Mature shrubs don't really need winter protection, but go ahead and pile the leaves around them anyway. Not only will this save you the work of bagging the leaves, but you'll be treating your shrubs to a wonderful meal of leaf mold. Fallen leaves make a good mulch for large plants like trees and shrubs. Remove any undecayed leaves in the spring, so they don't keep the soil from warming up.

Q. *When is the best time to transplant and add flowering shrubs to the yard?*
A. Early spring, around the time the crocuses bloom is a good time for adding or subtracting shrubs, but early fall is also good for the lazy gardener if autumn rains are expected to help with the watering. The secret is to move your shrubs and trees when it's cold enough to put them into hibernation, but not so cold that the ground is frozen. Remember to pamper any plant with extra water the first crucial year after a transplant.

Q. *Do I really have to pick off all the dead flowers from my rhododendrons, lilacs, and other flowering shrubs?*
A. No. Your shrubs will still bloom if you don't get around to removing all the spent flowers. You may not get as many blooms or as much new growth, but I've never

noticed a big difference between rhododendrons that were cleaned up after blooming and rhodies that went natural. Removing the old flowers is not only a tiresome, messy job, but, unless you do it carefully, you could break off the new tip growth on your rhodies and lilacs along with the spent flowers. If your shrubs are large and viewed from a distance, then the fading flowers should be left alone to die a quiet death. Save your precious time and energy for more crucial gardening tasks.

CHAPTER FOUR

Bulbs: Fancy Flowers without the Fuss

Formal, fancy, and flagrantly colorful flowers grow from bulbs. Bulbs can give you beautifully simple blooms in all the pastel colors of spring tulips. Bulbs can also dazzle the yard with the vibrant oranges and yellows of summer-blooming gladioluses and begonias.

Actually, some of these flowers grow from bulblike corms and tubers, but we'll just call them all bulbs in this chapter. No sense getting bogged down in details when there are gardening shortcuts to be learned.

Lazy gardeners can rejoice and relax because, once you plant a bulb, the work is over. No need to water, feed, or prune back a hearty bulb in bloom. Just think of the bulb as the underground supply center for the flower. The food for that flower is already stored in the bulb. All you have to do is dig a hole, plant, and wait. Bulbs are nature's very own ready-to-go, pre-fertilized, and pre-measured flower-growing kit.

Just remember the rule for any lazy gardening plant: Don't fight Mother Nature. Choose only the bulbs that are easy to grow in your soil and climate. The lazy way to research this is to see what pops up in your neighbor's yard. Some bulbs like grape hyacinths and windflowers spread and multiply so easily that, if you admire them aloud, you'll probably get sent home with a freshly dug clump of your own. Gardeners are generous with easy-to-grow plants.

If you're an extra-lazy gardener, then plant only hardy bulbs that can stay in the ground all winter. Tender bulbs that bloom in the summer, like dahlias, tuberous begonias, and gladioluses, demand more attention. These tender bulbs need to be dug up and stored each fall before the ground freezes. Summer bloomers may also need fertile soil and more water than spring bloomers, which are winter-hardy and easier to ignore. The bulbs that bloom in the spring are also more likely to naturalize. This means they will return without replanting each year and eventually multiply into large colonies. A single bulb that likes the feel of your garden can grow into a large clump of carefree blooms after only a couple of years.

When to Plant Bulbs

If you want flowers in the spring (tulips, daffodils, hyacinths, etc.), then plant the bulbs in the fall.

If you need summer color, then plant the bulbs of gladioluses, tuberous begonias, and dahlias in the spring. These bulbs are afraid of freezing weather, so plant them after the last spring frost.

If you're too lazy to research what to plant when, just walk into a garden center when you get the urge to plant a few things in the ground. You'll see a display of bulbs set up with pictures of the flowers that will bloom. Bulbs are sold by your local garden center at the time of the year when they should be planted. Go ahead and get carried away. Plant a little bit of everything the first year, so you can judge for yourself what does best in your yard. You're sure to get flowers from just about any bulb the first year. It's only if you want bulbs that will naturalize and return year after year that you have to be choosy about what you plant.

You'll find plenty of free and accurate planting information at your local garden center or in a mail-order catalogue that sells bulbs.

How to Plant Bulbs the Lazy Way

■ Sort your bulbs into groups of seven to twelve. All the bulbs in each group should be the same type and same color. Use large plastic sandwich bags to keep the groups separate.

■ You can skip the sorting stage if you buy your bulbs in presorted packages. Bulbs are often sold in packs of twenty-five at garden centers.

■ Use a big shovel, not a tiny trowel, and dig one community hole for each group of bulbs. One hole for the yellow daffodils, another hole for the red tulips, etc.

■ Go ahead and cheat if you don't feel like planting the bulbs as deep as it recommends on the package. If you live where the winters are mild, you can get away with planting your tulips and daffodils four to five inches deep rather than the eight to twelve inches that is usually recommended. I quit worrying about the planting depth years ago when I grew too lazy to dig down any deeper than one scoop of the shovel. In our mild winter climate, my bulbs bloom their happy-go-lucky heads off even when buried a shallow three inches deep.

■ If you need the extra winter protection of deeply planted bulbs but you're still too lazy to dig a hole one foot deep, you can get away with digging a shallow hole, but only if you mound extra soil or leaves three or four inches thick on top of the planting area. A mulch of fallen leaves makes a wonderful bulb blanket. Pile a little soil on top to keep the leaves in place.

■ Once you've got your hole dug, check out the soil. Bulbs will rot in wet and soggy ground. If you have sticky, wet, or clayey soil, add peat moss and sand to the planting hole. If improving wet soil is too much of a bother, then don't waste your time planting bulbs in the ground at all. Pot them up in containers or build raised beds with sandy soil instead. Don't even try to argue with Mother Nature on this one. Bulbs insist on well-drained soil.

■ You may have read that bulbs need bonemeal or fertilizer mixed into the soil at planting time. You can skip this step. All the food your bulb needs to flower the first year is already stored inside of it. Gritty bonemeal and special bulb foods are fine for the fanatic, but the lazy gardener will still get lovely blooms without fertilizing — for the first year, at least.

■ Once the hole is dug, dump all the bulbs of one group into the community hole. No need to get on your hands and knees yet. Just lean on your shovel as you toss the bulbs from your plastic bag.

■ Now you can squat and arrange the bulbs so that they're all sitting on their round little bottoms, with their pointy noses sticking in the air. Space them far enough apart, so that they don't spend the winter rubbing shoulders with one another. You may have to widen the hole a bit at this time. The experts will tell you to leave a three- to six-inch space between each bulb, but that means you would have to dig a bigger and wider hole, and waste more of your precious energy. I cheat. I plant them closer, and I always get away with it.

■ Fill in the hole with the soil, but reverse the order when you fill. Put the rich, dark topsoil into the hole first so this will be closest to the bulbs' roots. What was on top should now be in the bottom. Spread mulch on top if you need the extra protection from freezing winters or a shallow planting.

■ Don't water, don't worry — just wait. If Mother Nature intends for bulbs to bloom in your yard, then you'll see success the very first year.

More Maneuvers for Maximum Impact

Here's how to design with various kinds of bulbs to get the maximum return on your energy investment:

■ Plant different types of bulbs, close to one another, but use the same colors to make a bold statement. A clump of yellow daffodils and a dozen golden tulips multiply the color magic. Try pink hyacinths with pink tulips. For maximum impact, make sure your color partners bloom at the same time.

■ Use two or three groups of bulbs, but use only two contrasting colors. Red and yellow tulips or purple and white crocuses stand out more vividly than a huge collection of pastels. Put blue grape hyacinths with your yellow daffodils.

■ Put the early spring bloomers close to the house or along the path you take every day to your car or mailbox. The low-growing crocus and snowdrop bulbs are better appreciated up close. Save a spot for these small but early bloomers next to your front door.

■ Look out your favorite window and focus on a place for spring bulbs. Rainy spring days may keep you indoors, so plan ahead for a blooming view.

■ Plant tall tulips and other floppy flowers where they'll be protected from the wind. Situated between two large shrubs or against a wall are smart choices. Lazy gardeners never run out to prop up fallen flowers.

■ Use tiny, delicate bulbs in containers or window boxes, where they'll be closer to eye level. Miniature daffodils in the spring and dwarf dahlias in the summer look just right in small pots or blooming in shallow window boxes.

■ Bulbs planted against a solid background won't get lost in a busy landscape. A fence or evergreen shrub makes a fine background for showing off tall tulips or glads. Low growers like dwarf tulips or crocuses stand out near a piece of pavement or patio for contrast.

■ Any place where there's a large rock emerging from the ground is a perfect spot for a clump of bulbs. The smooth texture and light color of a boulder magnifies the delicate beauty of your bulb blooms. Remember the lazy landscaping tip from Chapter One and use lots of rocks and boulders in your yard's design. Then you'll have lots of places to tuck in a few bulbs.

■ Summer-blooming bulbs like dahlias and gladioluses that grow tall are easiest to grow alongside a fence — use sticks or stiff wire to prop them up against the fence when they bloom.

Choosing Tulips for the Lazy Landscaper

Tulips are the world's favorite of all spring-blooming bulbs, but lazy gardeners must choose wisely if they intend to tiptoe through the tulips without tiring out.

■ The shorter, the better. Low-growing tulips are tidier, since they don't flop over in the wind or from spring rainstorms. Dwarf tulips are also more resistant to summer drought.

■ Many low-growing tulips bloom early in the spring, when you really need the color. Lots of shrubs are outblooming each other with flowers in May, but choose a March-blooming tulip and it will have the stage all to itself.

■ More than any other reason, choose short-stemmed tulips, because they multiply, naturalize, and return each spring more dependably than tall ones.

■ Seek out the low-growing or dwarf tulip varieties listed at right. They have many different common and scientific names, but all were meant to spend their lives reblooming every spring for truly lazy gardeners.

More Bulbs for the Lazy Gardener

Try these five bulbs for many happy returns. They naturalize easily and will rebloom year after year, even if ignored.

Daffodil: The smaller varieties that bloom in clusters, or the hardier types commonly called narcissus are the daffodils that are easiest to naturalize. These easy-growing varieties also bloom earlier in the spring then the taller, showier daffodils.

Autumn Crocus: If your yard looks rather drab in autumn, tuck a few bulbs of a fall-blooming crocus around shrubs and in borders. The spring-blooming crocuses are also lazy-gardener bulbs. Both types of crocus are planted in the fall and, because the bulbs are small, you don't have to dig a very deep hole. Just bury the crocus bulbs three inches deep and you'll have years of dependable blooms.

Hardy Anemone blanda: Sometimes called "windflower," these spring-blooming bulbs will grow in any soil as long as it is well drained. They multiply rapidly. What I like most about blanda is the foliage. The leaves are low, dainty, and compact, so when the flowers die back you still have a month or two of green groundcover.

Hardy Cyclamen: This is another bulb that will bloom during the autumn or very early spring. These are exotic-looking creatures and closely resemble the delicate florist's cyclamen. The difference is that the hardy cyclamen will survive in dry, rocky soil and spread naturally into larger clumps. The pink-blooming cyclamen in my garden blooms spring and autumn and even thrives in the crummy soil under the fir trees. The hardy cyclamen does not need winter protection in mild winter climates. Like the windflower, it has low-growing, attractive foliage.

Wood Hyacinth or Scilla: These are the spring-blooming bluebells that grow wild in many parts of the country. Plant a couple bulbs and forget about them. You'll have a lifetime of blue blossoms. These are taller than the more purple grape hyacinths, but the two are often confused because they share the same easy-going tempera-ment and an uncontrollable urge to reproduce themselves. Watch out for all this blue enthusiasm. Given ideal conditions, either of these bulbs will take over your entire lawn and garden and turn into uncontrollable weeds. This could give a meticulous gardener a depressing case of the blues. The leaves of scilla get yellow and sloppy after the flowers fade, so plant this bulb where you can hide the dying foliage.

The Story of the Top Five Bulbs

I admit to having a personal preference for the five bulbs mentioned above. This tale should convince skeptical gardeners that some bulbs will bloom for years when neglected.

When I was in high school, my family moved from town to a big farmhouse out in the country. My parents wanted to raise their large family where there was room to grow. We had been living in a suburb and "planned parenthood" was just becoming popular. Now, my folks planned their family, of course — they just planned on a baby every year, and stuck pretty much according to plan. After seventeen years of marriage, there were fifteen children. We needed more room.

Moving from our huge custom-built home with the lovely yard to a paint-peeling farmhouse with knee-high weeds was not a move us older kids looked for-ward to. The farm had been neglected for years, and the overgrown landscape was just one of the needed improvements. We settled in for the winter expecting nothing but more weeds from the yard in the spring.

It was in February that the front lawn burst into bloom.

There were flowers sprouting up around huge trees and beneath overgrown shrubs. The lousy lawn sported lovely crocuses, followed by drifts of daffodils. Scilla bloomed in clumps of lavender and blue. Windflower wove its colors down the path to the aging barn, and hardy cyclamen sprouted under rusty farm machinery. Here was a garden where the bulbs had been liberated by neglect. They went wild, producing a profusion of blooms that had increased every year. By spring, we all began to like the old place.

The bulbs weren't the only thing producing and increasing. My Mom had her sixteenth and last child that same year, and taught us all to bloom where we were planted. But that's another story.

How to Hide the Dying Foliage from Your Blooming Bulbs

After the beauty of the flower comes the ugly decay of the bulb's foliage. Daffodil leaves will lie down, yellow, and decay in a deathly sprawl. Tulip leaves will turn pale and blotchy but persist for weeks. Even the thin, grassy foliage of crocus bulbs turns brown and dry as the leaves ripen. Now here's the problem. You cannot pull, trim, twist, or remove the unsightly foliage. The longer you leave it alone, the better your chances that the bulb will bloom again the following year. The dying leaves are sending energy underground to make next year's bloom.

■ One thing you can do to tidy up is to snip off the dead flower heads. This is easy to do on single-stem bloomers like tulips and daffodils. Just use your pinching fingers to decapitate the blooms of faded glory. Now, don't get overzealous and cut off the stems of the faded flowers. Headless tulips may look a bit strange, but the dying flower stem helps the leaves in making next year's blooms.

■ The tidiest way to deal with dying foliage is to dig up the offending bulbs, floppy leaves and all, and transplant them to an out-of-the-way spot. You have to dig the bulbs carefully to avoid damaging them and lift them gently from the ground so as not to snap off the leaves. Then these bulbs must be transplanted immediately. The whole affair is a lot of work, not recommended for lazy gardeners.

■ If you're more lazy than thrifty, you can chop off the dying foliage right at ground level. You'll then enjoy a neat and tidy yard, but have to replant with new bulbs each year.

■ Planting your bulbs in pots and then sinking the pots into the ground is often suggested as a way to enjoy spots of color in the spring. The problem with potted bulbs is that they rarely bloom well the second year. The roots just don't spread and support next season's blooms as well as bulbs planted directly in the ground. If the bulbs can't guarantee you a second year of encore blooms, you might as well stick your bulbs in the ground and then prune off the dead leaves. It's a lot easier to toss out the bulbs and replant each spring than it is to dig up a submerged pot and then find a spot to store the potbound bulbs through the summer.

■ Low-growing and very small bulbs are better candidates for growing in pots when a second year of bloom is your goal. You can pot up delicate snowdrop or crocus bulbs and usually get several years of flowers out of them before they fade away. Just plant annual flowers in the pot to hide the dying foliage after these small bulbs bloom.

The committed lazy gardener will simply plant the bulbs, enjoy the blooms, and ignore the dying foliage. Here are some ways to make the mess less obvious:

■ Plant taller-blooming flowers behind a large rock. When the flowers are at their best, they will peek up behind the stone. Then, when the foliage dies back, it can age in private behind the stone curtain.

■ Before your bulbs even bloom, plant low-growing flowers amongst them. Annual flowers like alyssum and pansy will fill in to hide the dying bulb foliage later on in the season.

■ If you have an area with groundcover plants, you can interplant bulbs and then watch the flowers poke up and bloom through the groundcover. The unsightly foliage will then be less obvious, surrounded by groundcover plants that help to mask the mess. Vinca minor, or periwinkle, is an excellent groundcover to use with bulbs.

■ Create a lovely scene that can be enjoyed from a distance. Use mass quantities of daffodils or crocuses, which naturalize easily, but plant them far away from the house for long-range enjoyment. When the foliage yellows and dies, you'll hardly notice the mess out there on the horizon.

■ Plant spring bulbs beneath and around your flowering shrubs. Early bloomers like crocus and dwarf tulips will really stand out near shrubs that lose their leaves in the winter. By the time the bulbs are done flowering, the shrubs will have blossoms or leaves and will attract the eye's attention away from the fading foliage of the bulbs below.

■ Plan so that later-blooming bulbs and flowers will bloom in front of earlier bulbs that are past their prime. Use crocuses or snowdrops in the back of your flower bed and then plant a group of early tulips in front of this, with later-blooming tulips or daffodils in front of the early tulips. After the last group of bulbs has bloomed, leave room at the very front of the border for geraniums or begonias. These two summer annuals can be purchased as good-sized plants in late spring and both make a nice border for blocking the bulb bed from view. It's easy to shield the eye with progressive plantings when you have a bed that is only viewed from the front. You have to plan more carefully with beds that are viewed from all directions.

Most-Asked Bulb Growing Questions

Q. *I planted daffodils and was pleased to see plenty of fat yellow buds ready to bloom. Overnight the buds and some of the leaves were attacked. Holes were eaten in the leaves and petals were completely eaten off of the blossoms. What kind of insect did this damage?*
A. Slugs and snails work fast to devour daffodils, which they consider a gourmet feast. A single daffodil blossom will attract dozens of slugs for a midnight feeding frenzy. The only tip they leave after the meal is a silvery trail of slime. Every daffodil should be protected from slugs as soon as the leaves emerge. Use a commercial slug and snail bait or set out saucers of beer near your daffodils for the slugs to fall into and drown.

Q. *There is something wrong with my tulips. The flowers are splotchy and the leaves look stunted and pale.*

A. It sounds like the symptoms of botrytis rot on your tulips. This is a fungal disease that is sometimes present in the soil but more often brought in on new bulbs. Any lazy gardener with disease-ridden bulbs should dig up the flower, bulb and all, and throw it away. Then check to make sure your soil drains well and buy your replacement bulbs from a reliable dealer.

Q. *How do you tell if the bulbs you buy are of good quality?*
A. The bigger, the better when it comes to buying bulbs. Small size is often the reason some bulbs are sold at bargain prices. Small bulbs can still be healthy, but they may take an extra year of growth before they bloom. The larger Number One grade bulbs are much preferred by lazy gardeners who want bulbs that will naturalize. Healthy bulbs feel solid, not light and hollow. The skin should be free of cuts or blemishes and never show signs of mold growth. Don't worry if the outer skin, or *tunic*, of the bulb is loose and peels off easily. Healthy bulbs aren't a bit shy about losing a bit of covering.

Q. *I planted a hundred daffodils to naturalize in my field, and everything went along as planned for a couple of years. The flowers increased in number and the clumps grew larger. This spring, however, I noticed fewer flowers but lots of green foliage. Do you think moles are eating my daffodils?*
A. Don't blame the moles — they are meat eaters and feed on worms and grubs, not bulbs and roots. Mice and other rodents find daffodil bulbs offensive, so the problem is not theft, but rather overproduction. Over the years, many bulbs will reproduce to the point where they are growing too close together and all they can muster is foliage without flowers. You can dig and separate your daffodil bulbs, but wait until after the foliage has yellowed. Separate any baby bulbs from the mother bulb, but don't force apart any double-nosed daffodils that have developed a strong attachment. If you want to avoid doing this job for a good many years, than take the time to space the bulbs eight inches apart and bury them eight inches deep. Deeply planted bulbs don't multiply as rapidly. If this sounds like too much work, just buy more large daffodil bulbs and replant all the clumps every three or four years.

Q. *My gladiolus blossoms have streaks in them and the leaves have yellow stripes and tiny holes. Is this a disease of some type?*
A. Think thrips, not disease, when you see yellowing foliage on gladioluses. Thrips are tiny insects that stunt and distort flowers and leaves by sucking the juice out of glads. Clean up your glads in late summer by cutting them close to the ground. If you're lucky, the thrips won't survive the winter, and you can try again next year. If thrips return to your gladioluses year after year, stop growing glads. The control of thrips takes persistence and poison and is not a job for the lazy gardener.

Q. *How do I get rid of millipedes from my dahlia bed? I dug up my dahlia tubers and found these insects eating my tubers.*

A. Let's get to the root of your dahlia demise. The millipedes are only feeding on rotting tissue, which is present because of some dahlia disease. Dahlias rot easily in cold, wet soil, so raise your beds and add sand and peat moss to the soil to keep them healthy. Dahlias are beautiful flowers that bloom in late summer when most flowers start to fade. They also need rich, porous soil and are sensitive to freezing weather; the taller types need staking and tying. If your dahlias are rotting, then throw away the bulbs and consider whether Mother Nature really meant for dahlias to grow in your soil. Try growing daylilies instead.

Q. *I love tuberous begonias for my shady patio, but this year, after the plants seemed well established and looked ready to bloom, they just toppled over and died. They showed signs of wilting a bit just before they took their death dive.*
A. Tuberous begonias commit suicide for several reasons, most often because their roots rot. They need plenty of peat moss in the soil to maintain moisture and should not be overwatered. There is also a weevil that feeds on the bulb until it totally destroys its root system. You can avoid both of these problems by potting your tuberous begonias in sterilized potting soil every spring. Sterilized soil is sold by the bag at garden centers. Give these plants plenty of elbow room. Tuberous begonias are antisocial and hate to touch leaves with other plants.

CHAPTER FIVE

I'll Promise You a Rose Garden If . . .

Even if you're a lazy gardener, I can promise you a rose garden. There are some roses that gobble up fertilizer, bug spray, and lots of time, but there are others that just don't deserve this fussy reputation. To successfully grow the easy-care roses that are now available, you need only to keep these three simple promises:

1. Promise to plant your roses in well-drained, fertile soil.

2. Promise to pick a spot where they will get at least a half day of full sun and good air circulation.

3. Promise never to let them go thirsty. Roses need water. Lots and lots of water.

Now, before you make the triple pledge and run off to place your order for fifty assorted rose plants, you've got to finish reading this chapter. Some roses will wither away even if you keep the above promises. Some roses will grow tall and scrawny without careful pruning. Some roses will be cloaked with disease without weekly spraying. Some roses will barely bloom without a lot of fertilizing. Some roses you should definitely do without.

The roses for the lazy gardener are those that adapt well to whatever Mother Nature dishes out. The best roses for laid-back gardeners are the old-fashioned species roses, the hardy polyanthas, the floribundas, and disease-resistant shrub roses. The lazy gardener must be very picky about rose varieties, or he or she may be burdened with a very picky rose.

Allow me to introduce you to the best behaved roses in the business. This collection of roses for the lazy gardener wasn't compiled from my experience (and rose failures) alone. I went right to the experts. I don't mean the American Rose Society, or any professional organization. The experts I polled are average gardeners first, and rose growers just as a matter of coincidence. These rose growers put ease of care first, and color, form, and size of bloom second. These are the roses that will perform under a no-pressure maintenance program. These are the rose varieties endorsed by hundreds of very smart but lazy gardeners.

The Top Five Roses for the Lazy Gardener

Shrub Roses: Bonica and Simplicity are the names of two shrub roses that get high marks for low care. Both of these roses will grow to five feet and bloom pink. They are covered with blossoms for most of the summer. Either would make a great hedge.

Polyantha Roses: The Fairy is the favorite low-growing rose of the lazy gardener. Like all polyanthas, The Fairy is adorned with small but numerous flowers, borne in clusters on short stems. This rose stands out from the rest because of its high disease resistance and dainty pink flowers that reappear all summer long.

Hearty Climbers: Improved Blaze wins the race as the hottest rose ever to ramble over a split-rail fence. Blaze is a climbing red rose that has been improved by modern rose breeders for a longer blooming season. Blaze can be easily trained to cascade over an arbor. Climbing Peace and Climbing Double Delight are other hard-to-kill climbing roses.

Species Roses or Old-Fashioned Roses: These are closely related to the wild roses that survive on total neglect in the fields. Some don't bloom for as long as modern roses, but many offer the bonus of winter color with bright red rose hips or seedpods. These roses are so hardy and vigorous that they are sometimes used as a groundcover. They do especially well when allowed to cascade over a sunny hillside. *Rosa rugosa* is a species that survives almost anywhere, even near the seashore, where it blooms in spite of sandy soil and saltwater spray.

Floribunda Roses: This family of roses gives you lots of small flowers that bloom in clusters. Europeana is a good example of an easy-care floribunda, as this rose grows short and bushy. Europeana blooms heavily, and its flowers are a classic rose-red color. Not only does this rose resist disease, but it is also tolerant of very cold and very warm weather conditions. A tidy rose with an easy-going nature.

The favorite varieties mentioned above should not deter you from trying some of the other roses in the same family. Most of the polyanthas, floribundas, species, and shrub roses are easy to grow. In your area there may be an even better variety choice then the example given. Just remember that the easiest-to-grow roses are not the formal hybrid teas with their long stems and gigantic blooms.

For some lazy gardeners, a month's worth of rose blossoms is all they expect, and good soil, good sun, and lots of water will ensure this minimal performance. There are three more promises you need to keep if you want any rose to do more than survive and honor you with a bevy of blossoms in June.

Promise to obey this next set of rules, and I promise you a rose garden of outstanding, long-lasting beauty. Roses that bloom all summer and well into the fall. Why, I'll even promise you a formal rose garden of long-stemmed hybrid tea roses. Hybrid tea roses are from a family that is harder to grow, but they have the largest flowers and seem to be the roses that most gardeners have in mind when they think of a rose garden. The three extra promises aren't hard to keep, and the reward for your extra efforts will be a rose garden that adds a lot of class but not a lot of work.

4. Promise to fertilize two or three times during the growing season.

5. Promise to prune your roses every spring.

6. Promise to protect your roses from disease and insects.

Make all six promises to your roses on the day you plant them and you both should live happily ever after. Now study these tips, so that keeping these promises will be a lot easier.

Tips for Easier Rose Growing

Promise #1: Good Soil

Roses hate to have wet feet in winter weather. If your soil is sticky and wet all winter, it will need improving before you plant a rose. All roses like soil that is loamy and rich with lots of organic matter. Improve your soil before you plant and you'll save yourself lots of work later on. In good soil, a rose plant can send out an extensive root system, and this helps any plant to more easily take care of itself.

■ If your soil drains well and seems decent enough, just add one shovelful of peat moss to every planting hole you dig for a rose. Add an equal amount of composted steer manure (you don't need a steer — it's sold in plastic bags at garden centers) and stir this mixture until well blended. If you have compacted, clayey soil, add some gypsum, a mineral that's widely used as a soil amendment. Gypsum also provides calcium for the soil.

■ If your soil stays wet in the winter, build raised beds with landscaping timbers or rocks and fill in with a topsoil mix at least one foot deep.

■ If there is standing water in the spot where you'd like to grow roses, then you really have a drainage problem. Install drain tiles and replace the wet soil with a sandy loam to a depth of two feet. This is a lot of work, so you may just want to forget about growing roses in this part of the garden. Put in swamp plants instead.

■ Keep your soil covered with a mulch of bark chips. Not only will this keep down the weeds, but, as the bark mulch rots and decomposes, it will improve the soil.

Wet soil is not the only enemy of lazy rose growers. Roses need a fertile soil with a wide range of micronutrients and minerals. Micronutrients are like plant vitamins. If roses don't get all their vitamins, they grow tired and stingy with their blooms.

■ The cheapest way to fertilize is to spread composted grass clippings, manure, and leaves on top of the rose beds every fall. The winter rains can then wash all the nutrients down to your rose roots by spring.

■ If you don't have a compost pile (and you really should, you know), then substitute packaged steer manure or mushroom compost.

■ If you inherit an old rose garden or need to replace a rose that is dead or sickly, be sure to remove at least ten shovelfuls of the old soil and replace with fresh soil before planting a new rose in that same location.

Promise to give your roses good soil and you can relax most of the year. Remember that any plot of ground, be it too sandy or very sticky with clay can be transformed into a garden of rich soil by mixing in organic matter. Lots and lots of organic matter. Also, as mentioned before, gypsum helps to improve compacted clayey soils.

Promise #2: Good Location — Sun and Air
Diseases and other rose enemies like to hang out in dark, damp, secluded hideaways. Give your roses the cleansing kiss of sunshine plus a gentle rinse with circulating air and you'll keep them clean of nasty habits. Pick the location for rose growing carefully. It will save you work later on.

■ Roses need to bask in at least six hours of sun a day. Morning sun is the best. You want the sun to dry up the morning dew quickly to prevent disease.

■ Pick a spot away from the hungry roots of trees and shrubs. Remember that roses have far-searching hungry roots of their own, but are too shy to compete for the daily nutrient hunt.

■ Locate your roses away from buildings, walls, and hedges, which can stop the flow of air around your plants. Good air circulation means a spot out in the open — for all the world to see.

■ Too much wind can dry out or freeze your rose plants. If you garden in windy territory, choose a spot sheltered from winter winds. A building or a clump of trees can serve as a windbreak.

■ Don't crowd. Roses get claustrophobia and are hard to walk around when planted too close together. Mother Nature equipped roses with thorns to remind us that they don't like their neighbors getting too close. Space hybrid tea roses at least two feet apart, so you can walk between the plants easily for picking and smelling. Roses also look better when not tangled up in each other's arms.

■ Choose a location where the summer color can be enjoyed. Why fuss over a plant that you never see? Next to the patio or driveway, or close to the front walk are two attention-getting locations fit for formal-looking roses.

Promise #3: Give Plenty of Water

You just can't have easy-care roses without easy irrigation. If you want your roses to keep blooming all summer long, then you'll need to keep watering them all summer. Set up a simple system for watering and you'll enjoy a lot more roses with a lot less work. Remember that a water-stressed plant attracts insects and disease in the same way a dying animal draws vultures.

This seems like a good place to branch out into a story. My own rose garden is small but happy, but it wasn't always that way. For years, I battled a disease called black spot on my hybrid tea roses — by the end of the summer, even the most disease-resistant varieties would start dropping leaves cursed by the dreaded black spot. Years ago, I relied on chemical sprays and powders to control the problem, but still my roses suffered from various diseases.

It wasn't until we installed a sprinkler system that the black spot disappeared. I had always heard that getting the leaves of rose plants wet was a mortal sin, but I allowed the sprinkler system to come on every other morning and soak the foliage anyway. I got ready for a full-scale outbreak of mildew, mold, and black spot. The nightmare never materialized. Instead, the black spot disappeared almost completely from my rose garden. I wondered if perhaps wetting the foliage washed away the disease spores. A little research revealed that the black spot got worse during hot, dry weather. When my roses suffered from a lack of moisture, their defense against disease was weakened, and the black spot could sneak right in and start the invasion. If the plants were never allowed to go thirsty, their dam against disease never sprang any leaks. This certainly explains why roses suffer from more disease problems during hot weather. This also explains why the lazy gardener needs to keep the rose garden well watered, or else waste time battling insects and diseases. The enemy finds wilted rose plants easy pickings.

■ Install an automatic sprinkler system that waters your lawn along with the roses. This is the ultimate in lazy gardening, and you'll have years of ease after the one-time hassle of installation.

■ Lay out a drip system or a leaky hose just below the surface of the soil around your roses. Connect a hose to your buried pipes and water without waste. A drip system delivers water slowly, and you won't lose moisture to evaporation.

■ Let the water run a long time and soak the soil to a depth of one foot. Longer, less frequent waterings are not only better for your roses, but they also require less energy from the rose grower. Soak the soil about once every three days during hot weather.

■ Keep a mulch on the ground to seal in moisture. Bark chips last a long time and look attractive around roses. Even with a mulch, though, you must water your roses frequently in the summer.

■ Plan ahead and wash the family car or dog next to the rose garden. The extra water can then run off into the rose bed rather than trickle down the drain or driveway.

■ Empty the kiddie pool into the rose garden at the end of a hot summer day.

■ Don't wet the foliage if at all possible. Wet leaves encourage more disease and more work. If your roses are watered from an overhead lawn sprinkling system (as mine are), then have your sprinklers come on early in the morning, so the foliage has a chance to dry off before nightfall.

Three Extra Promises for Extra-Special Roses

You must remember that the easy-care roses that will thrive with only good soil, sunlight, and water are the more casual species roses, shrub roses, floribundas, and polyanthas. These are the roses for laid-back gardening, and they have shorter stems and smaller flowers than the tea roses used in formal gardens.

The hybrid tea rose is the long-necked beauty that many lazy gardeners only dream about. This is the rose variety that blooms most of the summer with full-sized flowers that are perfect for cutting and displaying in a bud vase.

The tea rose is indeed a gorgeous specimen, improved by plant breeders until it has become the aristocrat of garden flowers. But the hybrid tea rose has been bred for beauty, not brains. This lovely-looking plant has a gluttonous appetite for food and water, and it attracts pests and diseases faster than more common plants. Some hybrid tea roses even have snobbish attitudes to match their fancy bloodlines; they need constant attention to avoid falling victim to one disaster after another.

Despite all their drawbacks, the forewarned lazy gardener can still enjoy a formal rose garden of hybrid tea roses. You must only promise to be particular when you choose these picky roses. Skip over descriptive phrases like bicolored, fragrant, and spellbinding color, and look for words like disease-resistant, dependable, and long-lasting when you read rose descriptions. Get started with this list of five easy-to-grow hybrid tea roses. These roses have tested well all over the country, but you should consult your neighborhood nursery for the names of other tea roses that excel in your particular climate zone

Five Fancy, Formal Roses That Do Well for Lazy Gardeners

PEACE (peach or pink variety)
MR. LINCOLN (red)
QUEEN ELIZABETH (a pink grandiflora)
TOURNAMENT OF ROSES (coral pink grandiflora)
HONOR (white)

Note: A grandiflora is a cross between a hybrid tea and a floribunda rose. It inherits the best traits from each parent.

Now get ready to make those three additional promises I mentioned earlier: to fertilize, prune, and protect. If you want healthy hybrid teas, you'll have to add these three vows to your list of promises to ensure a great-looking rose garden:

Promise #4: Fertilize

All roses are hungry plants by nature because they work so hard at blooming. The hybrid tea roses are even hungrier because they've been bred to produce large flowers all summer long. A single fall application of manure or compost is not going to satisfy the appetite of a hybrid tea rose. The fertilizing tips that follow don't just apply to fancy roses, though. You can certainly pamper your easy-care floribundas, polyanthas, and species roses with regular fertilizing and enjoy a bumper crop of blossoms for your efforts.

■ Use a granular plant food made for roses. Rose fertilizers have more of the extra vitamins and nutrients that roses require. Plant foods made for lawns or rhododendrons lack the right stuff.

■ Read the label on the fertilizer. Read it a second time. Put your glasses on and read the fine print. Then follow the instructions exactly. Following label directions gives lazy gardeners the best return on their energy investment.

■ Too much fertilizer can hurt your roses. They suck in the food too fast, and the foliage will look scorched or burnt. Remember that roses are greedy and gluttonous to a fault.

■ The quickest way to apply fertilizer is to measure the correct amount into your gloved hand and then simply toss the granules in the right direction.

■ Fertilize during rainy weather. Well-watered plants take in the food slowly and politely and you can skip the step about watering in the plant food after you fertilize. During a dry spell, you have to water well, fertilize, then water again. If you do fertilize in dry weather, wash off the plant foliage to prevent fertilizer burn. Never fertilize more plants than you have time to water in immediately.

■ The most important time to fertilize is in the spring. That's when you most feel like messing around in the garden anyway. Your cue to feed is when the new leaves begin to unfold. Then force yourself to fertilize again in July. Don't get carried away and fertilize roses in the fall. You don't want a lot of new growth getting nipped by the autumn frost. Of course, if you're a rose-growing perfectionist, you'll want to fertilize exactly as often as recommended on the label of the rose food. Most labels specify one dose every four to six weeks. If you're a lazy gardener, twice a year is good enough.

■ Be efficient. If you have a lot of roses, first sprinkle the plant food around all of them. Then get a rake and scratch in the fertilizer around each plant. Finally, water all the plants at once. You'll have too much wasted motion if you treat each rose separately and try to fertilize, rake, water, and then move on to another plant.

■ If you're really into gardening, you may have a sprayer that attaches to your hose and can be filled with liquid plant food. You may also know how to measure out the plant food and add the water to the spray attachment in the proper dilution recommended on the fertilizer. If so, go ahead and spray your roses with liquid instead of granular fertilizer. It takes a lot less time, there's no bending or raking, and the plants absorb the food more quickly through their foliage than they do via the roots. Lazy gardeners too lazy to learn how to use these simple hose-end sprayers should reconsider. Spraying on the plant food may seem like an awkward task at first, but it's a lot quicker way to feed plants once you get the hang of it.

Promise #5: Pruning Pointers

Most roses need some pruning to remove the old canes or stems that are weak and tired. This will encourage new strong canes to develop, which will bear more flowers with fewer problems.

Hybrid tea roses need a good pruning early in the spring or they will grow tall and ugly. In contrast, the old-fashioned species roses are best left unpruned for years.

If you plant old-fashioned roses, then remind yourself that they are the lazy gardener's rose and don't worry about pruning. If you grow hybrid tea roses, remind yourself to get out there every spring and massacre them. If you grow the polyantha, floribunda, or shrub roses (and if you're a truly lazy gardener, that's what you should be growing), then take a middle-of-the-cut approach and trim these roses back just a little, removing any very thin or damaged branches.

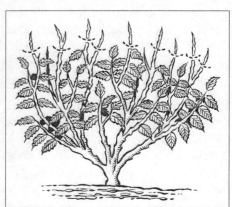

Some lazy gardeners act out of character when they're armed with a pair of pruning shears and approach the job with "shear enthusiasm." Severe pruning is recommended by rose growers who want only a few very large and perfect flowers. Mother Nature intended rose plants to have lots of branches and lots of flowers, so prune with restraint — you may get smaller flowers, but there will be lots more of them. Polyantha and floribunda roses with good form need only a slight haircut. Trim off the top one-fourth of these roses. (See illustration.)

Recite these pruning Do's and Don'ts before you arm yourself with a sharp weapon and attack the roses:

■ Don't panic. It's pretty hard to kill a rose plant just by making a mistake in pruning. In general, your goal is to remove a third of the ugliest stems (the stems that are dead, diseased, or damaged) and to chop off the top third of everything else that is left.

■ Do prune hybrid tea roses in very early spring, just before new growth begins. Depending on your climate this could be anytime from February to April.

■ Do leave five to eight canes, for hybrid tea roses, about two feet tall.

■ Do make your cuts at an angle, so that the stump left is slanted. Then you won't have raindrops sitting on the stumps collecting diseases.

■ Do use sharp instruments. The lazier you are, the sharper you should make your tools. Long-handled loppers are easiest to use on thorny roses, but hand pruners are fine if you have only a couple of plants. It's easiest to use a saw on thick old wood.

■ Do remember to spread a tarp on the ground to catch all your pruning crumbs. Rose clippings should be destroyed, not composted, since they can host insects and diseases. Remove any fallen leaves while you're at it.

■ Do keep the inside of the bush open for good air circulation. This means removing the new branches that aim towards the center of the rose bush. You want to strive for an open, vase-shaped plant. This is most important for hybrid tea roses. (See illustration.)

If you're a lazy gardener who hates getting bogged down in details, consider having a rose-knowledgeable friend or neighbor prune your hybrid tea roses for you. You might want to trade a couple of hours of lawn mowing or even baking in exchange for the pruning. Watch how it's done a couple of times and you'll soon feel confident enough to take over yourself.

Many nurseries and garden centers offer free pruning demonstrations early in the spring. Take advantage of these pruning clinics so you can observe up close how to prune correctly.

Promise #6 Protect from Pests

Most of your garden trees, shrubs, and flowers will fend off insect and disease problems all on their own, as long as they receive the food, water, and sunshine required for good health.

Hybrid tea roses, because of all the breeding they have undergone, have lost some of the natural defenses that older roses have against disease. During rainy or cloudy weather, many roses are susceptible to a disease called mildew. This white powdery fungus is first noticed on the new growth and buds. Black spot, rust, and viral diseases can also crop up, even if you never break a rose-growing promise.

Gardening books on rose care have all the answers if you want a written prescription for your problem. The lazy gardener without a library of reference books can just take a sample of the infected leaf to any garden center or nursery that sells roses. Local places are the best sources to consult because each part of the country has its own set of rose-growing problems and solutions.

If you notice a problem near the end of the summer, you can sometimes get away with ignoring the situation until winter comes and freezes away the enemy. Just make sure you clean up all the leaves and debris from your roses each fall. Sneaky diseases and insect eggs can hide out and survive the winter, protected in an old leaf.

Of course, lazy gardeners will want to avoid the mixing and spraying of chemicals of any kind. If you have a rose plant that insists on playing the victim to rust or black spot or that is always infested with bugs, then yank it out. This hard-hearted solution may seem cruel, but it's kinder than watching the disease-plagued rose wither away and die slowly. It's best to put a sickly plant out of its misery as soon as possible, before you grow attached to it.

Keeping a susceptible rose healthy can take weekly spraying and tedious hand-pruning. Every lazy gardener should know by now that it takes a lot of work to fight Mother Nature. The garden is no place for guilt. Out with the weak and sickly roses and in with the strong and disease-resistant varieties.

Here are other tips to keep your roses healthy and you away from the chemicals:

■ Throw the soapsuds left over from washing your car onto your roses. A mild soapy solution will actually skin aphids alive! The soap breaks down the waxy cuticle that covers an aphid's body, and the bug just dries up and blows away.

■ Plant your roses where you are forced to walk past them every day on your way to the mailbox or car. This will make it easy to take daily inspections. Squish a bug, remove a sick leaf, or pull a weed every single day.

■ Clip off the old flower heads of the flowers after they fade. This is a job that can be done at the same time you go to gather roses for indoor enjoyment. As long as you've got the clippers in your hand, you might as well remove anything that looks faded, spotted, or buggy. Pruning off a sickly leaf will nip any disease problems in the bud.

■ Load a bucket with your gloves, hand pruners, and a ready-to-use spray bottle of bug killer. The Safer Company markets a line of insecticidal soaps that will kill rose-eating insects. This company also makes an organic disease spray in a ready-to-use form. Now, take your bucket of supplies to the roses every time you visit. You'll get more done in less time if you have all your supplies with you. Use the bucket to cart away your clippings. A plastic garbage bag can also work as an efficient garden tote for rose supplies.

■ Add a birdbath or bird feeder to your rose garden. Birds eat bugs. You'll also be forced to inspect your roses more often as you make the trip to refill the feeder.

■ Prevention is the best protection, and there are several rose foods available that include a systemic insecticide, a bug-killing poison that is absorbed by the plant's roots. The plant is now poisonous to aphid and other sucking insects. Any time you can use one gardening product that does the job of two, you've saved yourself work.

■ More than anything else, choose disease-resistant, easy-to-grow roses and promise to provide them with proper sun, water, pruning, feeding, and soil.

Good Places to Place Good Roses

Now that you know how simple it can be to enjoy roses in your garden, you can use them in your yard to add class and color in more than the traditional ways. Think of the rose family as colorful problem solvers and consider them for these landscaping situations.

Too lazy to buy and plant annual flowers in your patio pots each year?
Pot up some miniature roses instead. Amber Queen is a tough miniature that will bloom all summer, even if grown in a pot. Just remember to be generous with the water and fertilizer, and your potted roses will live for years. Move all potted plants to a sheltered location during freezing weather.

Too lazy to build a fence for summer privacy?
Plant a row of shrub roses two to three feet apart instead. You'll not only have privacy, but flowers as well. A rose hedge grows faster than an evergreen hedge, and the thorny brambles discourage stray animals from wandering in. For a tall, sprawling, but very quick-growing screen, plant a row of sweetbriar roses. These roses grow to twelve feet in height, but you can keep them lower with annual pruning. Simplicity is the name of a simple-to-grow shrub rose with a more formal growth habit and large pink blooms.

Too lazy to tend a rock garden or mow a lawn on a steep slope?
Terrace the slope and plant roses instead. For a front yard, a formal planting of tea roses or dwarf polyanthas would look nice. Just be sure to include steps or a trail for easy access to your roses.

Too lazy to budget for a fine specimen plant to dress up your garden?
If you have an area in need of one spectacular landscaping shrub, plant a single rose plant. Choose a rose with a formal, upright form, one that has nice foliage and large flowers for the most spectacular effect. Queen Elizabeth is a pink grandiflora rose that looks regal when used as a focal point.

Too lazy to mow your huge lawn?
Remove a big hunk of the grass and put in a rose garden instead. If lawn care seems boring and monotonous to you, and puttering around blooming roses is more your idea of gardening, then a switch from lawn to rose garden might seem like less work. Be forewarned, though, that caring for even a small rose garden filled with hybrid tea roses is more time-consuming than the weekly routine of lawn care. It's also more rewarding.

Other Time-Saving Tips

■ Store your pesticides as close to the rose garden as possible. If you have a small arsenal of ready-to-use sprays close at hand, you'll use them at the first sign of trouble instead of procrastinating.

■ Choose bug and insect sprays from companies that promote organic products and you won't have dangerous side effects to worry about.

■ If you have a ratty-looking rose plant that has become tangled and overgrown, give it a chance at new life by whacking it back to short stumps in the early spring. Feed it lightly and water like crazy. If it doesn't recover beautifully after such serious surgery, accept that the operation was a failure and get rid of the patient.

Listen to Experience

The grayer the hair, the greener the thumb. Listen to senior gardeners, who may warn you of trouble with certain roses in your area. What may grow with ease in a climate with cool summers could be a spoiled brat growing in the heat of a southern summer.

I was warned not to buy a Sterling Silver hybrid tea rose years ago by a gray-haired gentlemen gardener, but I loved the luscious lavender color and fancy name of the rose. I went ahead and planted Sterling Silver in my rose garden anyway.

The rose bloomed (occasionally), the buds were lovely, and the color was really lavender — if the rain didn't make the petals rot or the sun didn't shine too hot. This lovely lavender rose also had the unforgivable habit of attracting diseases. After three years and maybe three perfect blooms, I replaced the tarnished Sterling Silver rose with a more dependable yellow variety called

Oregold. I may get yellow roses instead of lavender, but I don't spend the summer pulling disease-plagued leaves off of Oregold.

Oh, and by the way, it was a gray-haired gardener with a green thumb that recommended Oregold.

Most-Asked Rose Growing Questions

Q. *Help! There are tiny green bugs clinging to my rose bushes. They collect on the buds and new leaves and don't fly away even if I shake the bush.*
A. Your roses have been invaded by aphids, sometimes called plant lice. Aphids are sap-sucking free-loaders that are green and brown in color and prefer to set up housekeeping on the tender new growth of roses. The quickest way to handle an early infestation of aphids is to simply squish all the little buggers between your two pinching fingers. Aphids have soft, shell-less bodies and a gloved hand works as well as a chemical spray when you're in a pinch, so to speak.

If you have too many roses or too many aphids to squash easily, use soapy water or an insecticidal soap to spray the plants. As a preventive measure, use a rose fertilizer that contains a systemic insecticide the next time you feed your rose garden.

Q. *I have a rose plant that is always losing its lower leaves. First the leaf turns yellow and black spots appear, and the next thing you know the leaf falls off and another leaf begins to turn yellow. By the end of the summer I have a very bizarre-looking, almost leafless plant with a couple of rosebuds all alone at the top of the bush.*
A. You named the problem when you described the black spots that follow the yellowing foliage. Black spot is the name of a fungal disease that infects many rose plants. Prevent the problem by keeping the foliage dry and by removing every last leaf in the fall, to stop the infection from overwintering and returning next year. Keep your roses well watered during hot spells. You can spray with a rose-care fungicide to combat black spot, but you need to make frequent sprayings to keep ahead of this dark disease. Look for disease-resistant rose varieties that are less susceptible to black spot.

Q. *The leaves on my roses have a strange bumpy texture. The tops of some leaves are a mottled yellow, and on the undersides of the leaves you can feel the small orange bumps. Infected leaves tend to curl and wilt before they drop.*
A. Rust is ruining your roses. Rust is another fungal disease that can overwinter in fallen leaves, so make a thorough cleanup in the rose garden every fall. Those rusty orange bumps you feel are full of disease spores that are spread through the garden by the wind. Pick off every leaf that starts to yellow before the rust pustules get a chance to mature. A fungicidal spray will help in the battle against rust, and there are also rust-resistant rose varieties.

Q. *Is it okay to buy nonpatented roses? What about roses ranked Number One-and-a-half or Number Two?*

A. If you're a lazy gardener, then you had better invest in roses that work hard. This means buying only Number One grade roses. Every patented rose must be marked with a tag that has the patent number engraved. Newly developed roses carry a patent for the first seventeen years they are on the market. This doesn't mean that a nonpatented rose is a lousy choice. The rose might just be an old favorite and the patent has run out.

I once bought an nonpatented bargain rose at a K-Mart blue-light special. It turned out to be Handel, a lovely pink and white climber that is still one of my favorites.

Q. *When should roses be transplanted?*

A. New roses can be transplanted into the garden in early spring if they are bareroot, and anytime during the growing season if you buy them already growing in a pot. If you want to move a rose plant from one location to another, wait until the rose stops blooming in the fall, or move it in early spring as soon as the ground is thawed enough for you to dig a hole. Prune a rose back hard after transplanting.

Q. *What is a bareroot rose?*

A. Bareroot is how roses are described when they are offered for sale by nurseries in very early spring. The plants have no leaves and the roots are bare of soil. Usually the lower half of the plant is covered with sawdust and/or wrapped in a plastic bag to keep the roots moist. Roses ship easily in the bareroot or dormant state, so it is possible to purchase perfectly healthy roses by mail. Bareroot roses always come with complete planting instructions, and you should follow them exactly.

Q. *We moved to a house that is surrounded by overgrown rose bushes. I have no idea what kind of roses they are. How and when do we go about controlling these thorny monsters?*

A. Overgrown roses can be pruned at any time. Cut them way back to three-foot stumps and see what happens. Sometimes neglected roses aren't worth saving because they have become infested with disease. A severe pruning and a good fall cleanup can give those rebel roses a fresh start. If they don't redeem themselves after a year of feeding and watering, yank them out and replace them with a well-behaved plant for up close to the house. If you're really worried about destroying the roses in question with a severe pruning, you can take a sample of your overgrown rose to a public rose garden and ask the expert to identify and make pruning suggestions. I figure if Mother Nature lets a plant get king-sized, it must be made of pretty tough stuff. A heavy-duty pruning shouldn't hurt an overgrown mystery rose.

CHAPTER SIX

Blooming Annuals for Summer Color

It's flowers that turn a yard into a garden. Food for the soul and blossoms for the bud vase, flowers inside or outside transform a house into a home.

The problem for the lazy gardener is that growing flowers takes a bit more time and energy than maintaining a tree or tending the shrubbery. The maintenance of your flower beds can still be kept to a minimum if you choose the flowering plants carefully. The blooming borders of your dreams don't have to turn into the high-maintenance monsters of your nightmares. You can have your flowers and free time, too.

The rules are the same for flowers as for anything else that grows in your low-maintenance garden:

■ Discover which plants bloom easily in your yard and plant lots of them.

■ Get ideas from the flowers that do well in your neighbors' gardens. Property close to yours will have similar soil and weather. When you happen upon a flowering plant that does well, reward it by planting more. A mass planting is more impressive then a hodgepodge of different flowers, anyway.

■ Don't fight Mother Nature. If wild foxgloves or wood violets spring up uninvited, don't weed them out right away. Welcome any flowering plant that appeals to you. What you should be weeding out are the flowering failures that looked great in the catalogue or garden center, but do nothing but demand attention in your yard.

■ Grow the flowers that you really love. It's not work to grow a plant you really love. It's just an enjoyable hobby. My mother-in-law has no time to garden — yet she somehow finds plenty of time to lavish on her beloved sweet peas. Sweet peas have some very admirable traits, but are not what you'd call a low-maintenance flower. To a real sweet pea lover, it doesn't seem to matter that they need string supports and a deeply-dug planting trench every spring. Fall in love with a flower and you'll find the time to love the labor.

The Two Kinds of Flowering Plants: Annuals and Perennials

There are two types of non-woody plants that bear flowers. One hangs out in the garden for years, usually dying back in winter and popping up again in the spring. These are called perennial flowers. Common examples of perennials are irises, lilies, and peonies. The next chapter is devoted to perennials. Bulbs are also perennials, but are usually considered in a class by themselves.

The other type of flower is called an annual. You plant it in the spring, it blooms all summer, and then it dies. Petunias, marigolds, and zinnias are common annual flowers. You can keep the two types of flowers straight by remembering that an annual needs to be replaced every year, just as a high school class annual is reissued fresh each June.

I suppose you're wondering why anyone would want a plant that dies after one year when you can grow flowers that live on year after year? The reason is that the perennials that return each year are not altogether perfect. They start out slowly in the spring, bloom for a few blissful weeks, and then gradually die off and fade away during the summer. Most perennial plants bloom for only a short period of time.

Now annual flowers — here are plants that live life in the fast lane! The seedlings start out as sweet green things in May, but they grow up fast and begin a summer party with a riot of color. Annual flowers bloom and carry on like a madman with only a few months to live. These plants sense their short lifespan and bloom like there's no tomorrow. It's easy to find young annual plants for sale in the spring, and the only real chore is transplanting them into the garden. You can expect lots of color, lots of excitement, and then a sudden winding down as the warm summer weather comes to an end and the autumn frosts cool down the party.

The lazy flower gardener should choose from the easiest-to-grow annual flowers for a carefree summer of continuous blooms. Here's why even lazy gardeners should consider adding some annual flowers to the landscape:

■ Growing annual plants gives you the freedom to change your mind, your color scheme, and your choice of favorites every year. Compare this with a blooming tree or shrub and the work it takes to move it when a change is needed.

■ Flowering annuals allow you to cram a lot of different flowers into a small space. Even apartment dwellers can experiment with four or five different blooming plants in just one pot. Small city gardens can host an amazing collection of blooming annual plants in just a small area.

■ Annual plants are inexpensive. The frugal gardener can enjoy a garden of flowers for the price of a couple of seed packets. Even a dozen started annual transplants will cost less than a single tree or shrub.

■ Some annual flowers add fragrance to the garden. Alyssum and flowering tobacco are good examples. Trees and shrubs may scent the garden, too, but flowers can be grown closer to the house or window, or even right under your nose in a pot on the patio.

■ Annual plants extend the blooming season. You've probably figured out by now that most trees and shrubs bloom in the spring, whereas most people spend time outdoors in the summer. Most annual flowers like to show off in the summer months, when you most appreciate the beauty of exterior decorating.

Good Places to Add Annuals without Adding Work

■ Bordering the lawn. If you outline the lawn with flowers that sprawl a little, you won't have to worry about edging the grass. Petunias are a good choice because they bloom even better if you nick them with the lawn mower. The floral colors will stand out against the green background of the grass, and the flowers will get watered whenever you soak the lawn.

■ Plant a flower bed along a pathway. The path to the front door is the obvious place to show off a little fancy floral work. Your visitors can't miss the display when you put the flowers right under their toes. A pathway garden also means that the flowers will be close and convenient for you to putter around in. You could even pull a few weeds or snip a few blossoms every time you step out the front door. Keep your feet on the path and you won't even have to get your slippers dirty.

■ Add a flower bed where it can be viewed from inside. The view that you see when sitting in your favorite chair or eating your supper should be a beautiful blooming scene. Plant large, tall flowers like snapdragons or sunflowers, or masses of flowers like marigolds and impatiens that are easy to see from a distance. Suddenly, the term "window garden" takes on a whole new meaning. A blooming view from every window.

■ Plant on terraced slopes or above retaining walls and rockeries. Not only will these spots have the good drainage that flowers love, but creeping and cascading blooms really show off when allowed to tumble over a barrier. Lobelia and alyssum come to mind when I think of annuals growing down hillsides or spilling over rocks and bulkheads. Hanging gardens have made handsome displays since the days of Babylon.

■ Interplant some blooming annuals amongst the vegetables or bordering the vegetable garden. Chances are this is one part of your yard that already has good soil and that gets watered and fertilized regularly. Plant some blooming soul food with your other food. Flowers don't need canning and freezing, but lots of flowers are edible (just as plenty of vegetables are beautiful). Mix them up. Pansies are an example of an annual that will bloom early, when the vegetable garden is still sparse in the spring. Pluck the pansy blossoms and add them to your salads when you're outside harvesting lettuce.

■ If you have a few rose plants, add a low flower border or blooming background. As long as you're out fussing over the rose plants, you might as well weed, feed, and water a small flower bed at the same time. Once again, an early-blooming annual like pansies or alyssum will give the rose bed some needed spring color.

■ Deck out the patio with plants, and plant more flowers near the deck. Flowers surrounding your outdoor sitting rooms are close enough to enjoy and convenient enough to tend to.

■ The best place of all. Plant your flowers in pots. A container garden near the front door to greet visitors and pots on the patio to decorate the backyard. Chapter Eight is devoted to flower gardening in containers.

Plant Here and You'll Regret It

■ Don't plant under large trees or next to huge shrubs. Unless you add a three-inch layer of topsoil or compost, your little flowers will be competing with giant roots for food and water. They'll lose the battle.

■ Don't plant on the side of the house that nobody ever sees. That's usually the side without any windows. Out of sight means out of control and outrageously high maintenance. Plant shrubs in these landscaping outposts instead.

■ Don't plant up close to the house under the eaves. Not only is the soil dry and lousy next to cement foundations, but the flower bed won't be seen from inside the house. Do you ever gaze out a window and look straight down? An exception is the front of the house, where you want to create a nice public garden. You'll see the flowers as you drive up to the house.

■ Don't be tempted into adding a flower border alongside a narrow driveway. If the foot traffic doesn't beat the plants down, the wandering wheels will.

■ Lazy gardeners shouldn't plant "secret gardens" of annual flowers on the outskirts of their property. A distant flower garden will be inconvenient to water and feed when it's too far away from the hub of things to enjoy. Even dedicated plant lovers tend to neglect the flowers out yonder in the outer limits. (Trust me.)

■ People come before plants. Keep your flowers out of the path of children or pets. Large roaming dogs and children's games are not compatible with a ground-level flower bed. Don't try an island of flowers in the middle of a lawn if you have people and paws romping about. This is just another example of why you shouldn't fight either human nature or Mother Nature.

Annuals the Easy Way — Started Transplants

Annual flowers that are sold in little plastic trays as young green plants are sometimes called bedding plants or started transplants. They got their name because they're often set into the ground five or six inches apart and soon grow together to form solid beds of blooms. One beginning gardener thought that bedding plants earned their nickname because you can plant them and then go back to bed and forget about them. Only in dreamland will you meet bedding plants that independent.

Here are ten of the easiest-to-grow annuals that are commonly sold as started transplants. Most are sold four to six plants to a pack, with the exception of the geranium starts, which are usually sold as single plants, often in four-inch pots.

For Sunny Spots

Marigold: A dependable bloomer and tolerant of lousy soil, marigolds are always a good investment, so long as you have a sunny spot to grow them in. The short varieties are called French marigolds, and they're easier to grow than the taller African marigolds. Hot weather doesn't bother marigolds, but lack of water does. Very easy to grow from seed, but the started transplants are cheap and available everywhere. Comes in warm yellow and orange colors.

Geranium: Plant breeders just keep on improving the geranium. The large flower heads and circular leaves give this plant a dignified, formal look that's perfect for pots or borders in the front yard. Just make sure the soil drains well and the sun shines on your geraniums for at least half a day and you won't have any problems. In mild winter climates, your geraniums may return for an encore performance, just like a perennial flower. There are other annuals with this perennial personality that we'll discuss later. Bloom colors are sizzling hot reds and oranges or soft salmons and pinks.

Petunia: The laziest way to get massive displays of flowers is to plant petunias. Petunias will even perform in arid desert climates if planted in the spring and fall. They love the sun, but the petunias in my garden bloom beautifully in a partly shaded bed. Buy young plants when choosing petunia starts and avoid skinny transplants already in bloom or bud. Pinch off the top inch of the plants after transplanting them to encourage bushy side growth. The double-flowering petunias are harder to grow than the single or grandiflora petunias; the trailing petunias work wonderfully in hanging baskets.

Alyssum: Low-growing and covered with tiny blossoms, alyssum is the perfect edging or border plant for the lazy gardener. There is sometimes a problem getting them out of their plastic packs and into the soil at their new home. Alyssum hates to be moved, so buy young plants without any blooms and water them well the night before you attempt the transplant. Keep as much soil around the roots of the new plants as you can when you transplant. Alyssum is another sun lover that adapts and blooms in a lightly shaded spot in my garden. The white variety seems the most vigorous, but alyssum also comes in rose, purple, and a reddish color.

Snapdragon: An old-time favorite that has been bred with better disease resistance, allowing it to qualify as a flower for the very lazy. The tall-growing varieties are great for the back of a blooming border; when you cut off the blooming spikes for indoor use, you'll be encouraging more flowers to form. Snapdragons will return (winter over) in mild climates, especially if you plant them close to the house in a protected spot. Look for young transplants, and don't crowd them any closer then six inches apart when you set them out in the bed. Most snaps won't need staking and come in a pastel mix of colors.

Zinnia: The tiny Thumbellina zinnias have been showing up as started transplants in many garden centers. Zinnias have always been colorful sun lovers that also love hot summers, but now the dwarf varieties can be easily transplanted from packs. Pinch off the top flower bud as soon as it forms to encourage bushy plants. Don't even try to grow a zinnia in a partly shaded spot and, when you water, avoid wetting the foliage. If you have to fight mildew on your zinnia plants, then say good-bye and plant another annual more tolerant of your moist climate.

For Shady Spots

Impatiens: Now here's an annual that actually prefers a little shade and blooms even in very deep shade. Frosty weather and dry soil are the two killers of this annual flower, so don't plant them outside too early and keep the watering can handy. One of the nicest things about impatiens is the way it cleans itself. The dead flowers just fall from the plants all on their own, so you don't have to spend time nipping and clipping these nicely shaped plants. If you buy impatiens plants that are a little bit tall and leggy, snip off the top half of the plants before you put them in the ground. Put the cuttings in a glass of water; after a few inches of roots form, you can plant the cuttings outside.

Lobelia: The annual form of lobelia tolerates sun and deep shade, and this is one annual that really excels in cool summer climates. Lobelia comes in a trailing form that is perfect for cascading over the edges of pots and rockeries; or grow one of the compact varieties as an edging plant. One of the bluest flowers you can plant, lobelia comes in light blue, dark blue, and blue and white combinations. No snipping of dead flowers is necessary, but you may need to cut these annuals in half around August to keep them blooming until frost.

Wax Leaf Begonia: This is another shade-tolerant flower that doesn't need constant pinching and picking to keep it clean and compact. There are also tuberous begonias, but they are more difficult to grow. The easiest-to-grow begonia has a waxy-looking leaf and small but numerous flowers. The foliage of this annual is often more colorful then the flowers. Wax leaf begonias are often sold as single plants in large four-inch pots, much like geraniums.

Pansies: These annuals will extend your blooming season because they flower earlier than the other started transplants you can buy. A little frost won't hurt your pansies, so put them in the ground when your daffodils start to bloom. A cool, moist soil supports the most pansy blooms, but you need to protect these tender flowers from slugs and snails.

Now don't you dare limit your flower gardening to these ten very common annuals. There are cosmos, calendulas, and dwarf dahlias that give just as much color for almost as little work. Ageratums, poppies, and salvias are a few of the other easy-to-grow annuals that look great when massed into large groups. The secret is to plant a variety of flowering plants the first year and see what does the best. Weed out the flowers that fade in your hot climate or mold in your moist climate. Each year promise to try something new — even one plant or some borrowed seeds of something you've never grown before. You may just discover an unusual annual that loves your climate, your soil, and your laid-back approach to gardening.

Growing Annuals from Seed

Starting seeds indoors in little pots on the windowsill is not a sport practiced by lazy gardeners. Most of the easiest-to-grow annuals are available as transplants and are so inexpensive that it doesn't pay to hassle with seeding.

But I must admit that there are some perfectly wonderful annual plants that don't transplant well, so you just can't find them growing in little plastic packs ready to set out in the garden. Retail outlets get in a rut offering the same well-known annual flowers as transplants spring after spring. Sweet peas, wildflowers, and some tall-growing annuals like cosmos come to mind as annual flowers you can't find as transplants. If you want these plants in your garden, you'll have to resort to growing them from seed.

Save on Work and Sow the Seeds Outdoors

The lazy gardener should avoid starting seeds indoors whenever possible. It's much easier to just sprinkle the seeds directly into the soil where they will live out their lives. Outdoor seeding means you get to skip all the heavy-duty stress involved with transplanting. I'm warning you in advance that good soil preparation is important, and, unless you already have perfectly wonderful soil, you're liable to work up a sweat digging in peat moss and steer manure to improve your soil before you seed annual flowers. Despite the time and energy it takes to grow plants from seeds, it can be a very rewarding experience. So dig in! Follow these steps for outdoor seeding success:

■ Prepare the soil where you plan to seed by hoeing or digging to loosen the top three inches of ground and adding organic matter (peat moss, compost, or steer manure), so the soil is light and fluffy. Use a rake to smooth out the top layer of soil.

■ Now read the instructions on the seed packet and don't try to plant the seeds any earlier than recommended. If the packet says "sow the seeds when danger of frost is past," then call the nearest nursery and ask when the last frost is predicted for your neighborhood.

■ If the seeds are very tiny, it will be tricky to plant them evenly. Mix some sand in the envelope to make shaking the seeds out easier.

■ Use the handle of your rake or hoe to draw crosshatched lines across the seedbed. Plant the seeds where the lines cross, and they'll be evenly spaced and easy to distinguish from the weeds. (Yes, you will have to weed around the seedlings if you plant flowers from seed.)

■ Barely cover the seeds as recommended on the package and, after watering them, very gently cover the area with sheets of newspaper or cardboard. This will seal in the moisture and keep out the birds, but only until the seeds sprout. Then they will need all the sun they can get, so remove the covering.

■ Watch, worry, and water over the seedlings daily, but don't drown them with too much moisture, especially if the weather turns cool. In a couple of weeks the seedlings will have a second set of leaves, called the "true" leaves. This is the sign that they've graduated from the fragile seedling stage. Congratulate yourself. Now Mother Nature can step in and take over while the young plants bulk up and prepare for a budding future.

Starting Seeds Indoors

In climates where spring comes late, seeds will need to be started indoors. The lazy gardener must promise to use a commercial planting mix especially formulated for starting seeds. A good growing medium absorbs some of the mistakes that laid-back gardeners make with watering (whether too much or too little) and lessens the chances for disease disasters.

■ The easiest way to grow seedlings is to use little pots made of compressed peat moss. Some peat pots are sold already filled with a planting soil, so the pot and the soil form one simple unit. Other types of peat pots are sold empty, and you'll have to add your own soil. Peat pots make transplanting very easy. You just dig a hole and set the pot and plant right in the ground. Peat pots are available at garden centers and through seed catalogues. (See the Source Guide on page 161.)

■ Seeds sprout or germinate much faster if they receive gentle bottom heat. Put your little pots on top of the refrigerator or dryer immediately after you plant the seeds. I set the peat pots into a muffin tin for easy transporting and watering. I never have time to bake muffins in the spring anyway.

■ When seedlings are grown indoors, they may suffer from lack of humidity, or not enough moisture in the air. Use plastic wrap to loosely cover your trays of seedlings. Don't let too much moisture build up under the plastic or the seeds could rot.

■ Water with the fine mist from a spray bottle. Assign this job to children whenever possible. The novelty doesn't wear off for a week or so. You can also fill the muffin tin with water and let the peat pots absorb it from the bottom up.

■ Remove your seedlings from the source of bottom heat as soon as they sprout. Now line them up on a sunny sill for the duration of their indoor imprisonment. Seedlings will grow long, tall, and weak if they don't get enough light.

■ Harden the seedlings off in late spring by introducing them to outdoor temperatures very gradually. Let them spend a few nights on a covered porch or patio before you toss them out into the cold cruel world for good.

Now, don't get carried away and start growing all sorts of flowering wonders from seed. You may lose your membership in the lazy gardener's club. Stick to growing only easy-to-germinate seeds that grow into easy-to-live-with plants. Here's a list of annual flowers that are so simple to grow, even a child could do it. This is not an idle boast, since all these flowers have been grown from seed by my own preschoolers.

Marigolds: You can take a tin can, punch holes in the bottom, fill it with soil, and scatter in some marigold seeds. Remember to water and they'll come up. I discovered this fact when I was ten years old.

Nasturtiums: The seeds are large and wonderfully wrinkled. I had a Sunday school class of three-year-olds that planted nasturtium seeds in paper cups half full of dirt — not potting soil. A month later we had a windowsill full of escaping nasturtium vines ready to send home for Mother's Day.

Sweet Peas: Start these outdoors in early spring. A little frost won't hurt sweet peas, so don't go to the extra work of starting them inside.

I love it when people break all the planting rules and bloom with success anyway. The rule breaker in this story was my mother-in-law, the sweet pea lover. She got a hankering to grow some sweet peas one summer. She didn't want to wait until early next spring. It was July, and she had a hard time finding any sweet pea seeds available for sale, but finally she located a leftover package of seeds and proceeded to plop them into the ground. Apparently no one told the sweet peas they weren't supposed to germinate if planted in the heat of the summer. They sprouted and even bloomed a bit before the first fall frost cut them down.

The sweet pea story is meant to encourage experimentation with seeds, not flagrant disregard for all the planting rules. Go ahead and scatter seeds about casually in the garden if you feel wild and daring. Seeds are inexpensive, so gamble a little. You may be pleasantly surprised at how much comes up. The plant-and-hope approach to seeding has worked for lazy gardeners when they use these very accommodating annuals:

- CALENDULA
- COREOPSIS
- BACHELOR'S BUTTON
- COSMOS

- ALYSSUM
- MARIGOLD
- NASTURTIUM
- SWEET PEA

Keeping Your Annual Plants Happy

As annual flowers, most bedding plants will bloom quickly after you set them into your soil and keep on flowering all summer long. There are a few favors you need to perform for these flowers. If you skimp on these chores, your plants will skimp on the blooms. Give them a little extra attention in these areas, and annual flowers will show their appreciation with an extra helping of blossoms. Just remember to:

1. Water when dry. It's especially important to water new plants when you first set them out and on hot summer days. Annuals in the ground may need daily watering, and flowers in pots may need water twice a day. A good reason to keep all flowers within hose reach.

2. Fertilize gently. Use a slow-release plant food the day you set in the flowers and you won't have to worry about feeding these plants for the rest of the summer. Osmocote is the name of a plant food that fertilizes for up to three months. Many professional growers use it and sell it. There are also fertilizers you mix with water and granular plant foods that you mix into the soil. Remember that, if you improve your soil and use a compost mulch, you won't have to fertilize at all. (More about compost and mulching in Chapter Nine.)

3. Pinch and pluck the dead flowers. Once you let an annual flower blossom die and form seedpods, it figures its duty is done, and the flower factories shut down so the seed assembly line can speed up. Keep those faded flowers picked and the plant will keep trying to complete it's life cycle. Some flowers take care of this job on their own, and you never have to remove spent blossoms. For example, impatiens, lobelias, and wax leaf begonias don't need deadheading.

4. Plant your flowers where they prefer to grow. Most annual flowers thrive in well-drained soil and a sunny location. If you have a shady spot, plant shade-tolerant annuals.

Picking Out Prime Plants

If you hope to get away with a little laziness, then you had better make sure your plants are the pick of the litter. When confronted with a greenhouse or parking lot full of plants, you need a few guidelines to help you weed out the weaklings:

■ Short and fat, not tall and skinny is the best shape for young bedding plants to be in. You want to look for squatty plants that will transplant easily into your soil.

■ Look for green plants, but don't chicken out if the plants you want look a little pale. Young plants start to turn pale from lack of light very quickly. Bedding plants that sit on the bottom of a display rack or in the shade of a storefront will green up quickly once you get them home and in the sunshine.

■ Bigger is not always better. Bedding plants are often sold six to each plastic pack, and the older, larger plants are the ones that have been sitting around the longest. These overgrown plants could very well be rootbound — the roots so crowded and tangled that they may not survive a transplant. Not all plants suffer from tight quarters, however. I've bought overgrown marigolds at end-of-the-season sales that transplanted easily to my garden soil. They quickly doubled in size as soon as they were given room to grow. Other plants, like impatiens and lobelia, are more difficult to transplant when rootbound. They droop and pout when separated from their planting mates and never seem to catch up. Petunias are another annual that needs to be transplanted when young and small — avoid skinny petunia plants already in bloom.

■ The bigger the pot, the bigger the value. A new trend at garden centers is to sell single plants in bigger four-inch pots. The roots aren't crowded together, and the plant can actually grow to blooming size and still survive a transplant. These big plants are perfect for the lazy gardener with more money than time to spend. You can easily fill a few pots on the patio or create a color spot in your yard with these instant flowers. Impatient gardeners will love the idea of setting out plants already in bud or bloom. Just make sure you harden them off for one or two days before introducing them to the great outdoors.

Annuals: Tucking Them Properly into the Bed

The most important part of any bed is the mattress. The most important part of a flower bed is the soil. The lazy gardener soon learns that you don't take shortcuts with your soil. This doesn't mean that all annuals require loose, rich, and fertile soil. Some sturdy flowers like nasturtiums actually bloom better in less-than-fertile soil. Most annuals, though, will bloom more and complain less all summer long if you take the time to work the soil before you stick in the plants. Now calm yourself. Just because I used the a gardening term with "work" in it, it doesn't mean you have to waste an afternoon with a plough and mule digging up the top two feet of your hard-packed earth. Annual flowers have shallow root systems, and they only have to survive for one year. Here's the easiest system I've figured out to plant a couple of flats of annual flowers. Speed became important to me when I realized I only had an hour or two of uninterrupted gardening while my children were napping. Maybe golf or tennis claims more of the free time in your life. Or maybe you'd just rather get the job done quickly so you can get back to the easy chair.

Speed Planting: Adding Annual Transplants the Efficient Way

1. Load your wheelbarrow or tarp with a bale of peat moss and a bag of steer manure. Throw in your gardening gloves, hand trowel, and fertilizer. I keep a bucket loaded with my gloves and trowel on a nail in the garage. (This keeps the mice from crawling into the fingers of my gardening gloves, but then, that's another story.) Fill up a watering can and add this to your wheelbarrow of supplies, unless the hose will be close to where you work. Speed planting means gathering everything you need together before you set out for the garden.

2. The flats of flowers should be taken from the covered porch or patio where you stored them for hardening off and set about the yard where you'd like them to grow. This placing process involves dropping off the plant packs in the general area where they will be planted, but not removing any plants from their packs yet. You want to wait until the last minute to remove the plastic pack and expose the roots.

3. If you need to beef up the soil before you do any planting, add two shovelfuls of peat moss and one of steer manure to each two-foot square of the planting bed. Toss in a handful of dry plant food. Now mix the soil additives and your existing soil together with your hand trowel. You are improving just the area that the plants will go into, not the entire garden bed. Dig six little holes, or just enough for the number of plants in your pack. The little name tag that identifies the flowers you bought should tell you how close to plant them. If not, space the holes six inches apart.

4. You have now prepared a small area of soil and are thinking about adding the plants. Are they well watered? Don't try transplanting a dry annual. To get the plant out of its root-stuffed package, rip the plastic with your fingers or turn the container completely upside down and bang the corner against your bucket or wheelbarrow.

Never pull a plant out by its stem.

5. Each packet may contain four to six small plants. Rip the plants apart with your fingers, trying to give each plant as many roots as possible. Now set them in the predug holes and firm the soil around each plant.

6. This is the time to harden your heart and pinch back any little flowers trying to bloom prematurely on your transplants. You want to direct the plant's energy into root production instead of flower power at first.

7. After you fill one area with plants, water them in before moving to another section. Avoid transplanting on a hot day — it makes you and the young plants much too thirsty. Evenings are best for transplanting work.

8. Clean up the job site as you go by stacking the empty trays into one another and then tossing them onto your work tarp or wheelbarrow. Use that trowel to slice up any slugs and bash any bugs you come across while planting. Be sly and bury the murdered bodies — they'll rot and improve your soil.

9. Don't wait too long before you add a mulch around the young plants. Weeds will move into any plot of ground you leave naked and exposed. See Chapter Nine for more mulching details.

10. Some gardeners like to protect their newly planted annuals with newspaper tents the first few nights. If it makes you feel kind and generous, go ahead and blanket your sweet young things. I much prefer to just wait an extra week or two after the last expected frost. Annuals set out too early in the spring won't grow until it warms up, anyway. Might as well let the greenhouse grower fuss over them while you wait for the weather to warm up.

The Best of Both Worlds: Annual Flowers that Reseed Themselves

Ask a lazy gardener about alyssum and you'll always get a smile. There's also nicotiana, nasturtiums and poppies. Pansies and violas in some gardens and even petunias and lobelia in others. These are all annual flowers that return each spring without replanting.

Only a lazy gardener gets to enjoy reseeding annuals. The clean fiends who spend too much time ripping up dead plants and raking away garden debris will miss out on nature's plan of perennial annuals. You've got to let your garden ripen a bit in the fall. Leave the frost-blackened annuals in place over the winter and learn to appreciate their icy silhouettes and frosty forms.

I learned about reseeding annuals the hard way. A lovely border of white and purple alyssum was planted alongside the path to our front door in our first house. Since alyssum stays low and blooms all summer, it made a nice front border for the taller flowers I also planted. I bought the alyssum as young transplants, but soon realized that this is one annual that doesn't transplant well when rootbound. Only the very small plants survived the move. The big blooming alyssum plants were just too rootbound to make the transition.

As that summer progressed, so did the alyssum border, until finally, by August, the plants had grown together in a mass of purple and white edging that spilled politely over the edge of the pathway. It was lovely.

When the fall freeze hit and the annual flowers froze, I made a big mistake. I just wasn't busy enough to ignore the blackened mess, so I spent an afternoon diligently cleaning out the flower beds. This meant ripping up the dead alyssum plants and raking the flower bed smooth and neat. I wasn't even smart enough to spread a mulch on the soil. I thought the exposed soil looked neat and tidy.

There was one little alyssum plant I left alone. It was at the very edge of the border and smaller than all the others. Since it wasn't making a nuisance out of itself, I ignored it.

Spring returned, and I anxiously searched the garden centers for very small alyssum plants to transplant into my border again. We wanted to repeat the success of last summer's edging. The only problem was finding plants that were young enough. Rather than risk getting stuck with the large rootbound plants that failed me the previous year, I bought a pack of alyssum seeds and decided to be thrifty. The seeds were planted, the seedlings came up, and then a cold spell hit. All my little alyssum plants froze out and died — except, what's this I see sprouting forth from beneath the remains of last year's alyssum plant? Tiny seedlings that looked identical to my ill-fated alyssum crop were hiding beneath the dead skeleton of last year's plant. That forgotten alyssum had died all right, but the brave mother plant was protecting her babies with her lifeless skeleton. The seeds from her ripened flowers had germinated and then survived the cold spell because the mature alyssum had been left to sit all winter the way Mother Nature intended.

You can make up your own happy ending in your garden with rows and rows of alyssum that return to gracefully edge your borders every year. Just let your alyssum plants sit out the winter, then enjoy the seedlings the following spring.

Many annual flowers will reseed themselves in mild winter areas if you follow these guidelines:

■ Resist the urge to clean up and pull out every frozen annual.

■ You don't need to let all your plants ripen and go to seed, since one plant can give you numerous seedlings. Choose the mother plants in the most protected locations.

■ Scatter a bit of leaves or other loose mulch on top of your mother plants as the weather turns cold.

■ In early spring, check for signs of seedlings, but do not remove the dead mother plants yet. They may still offer protection from late frosts.

■ When the new seedlings have two sets of leaves (usually by the time the last frost has hit) you can safely remove the dead mother plant.

■ Now you can transplant the seedlings so that they are spaced from four to six inches apart. If you have an overabundance of new plants, just pluck out the extras, until you're left with evenly spaced seedlings.

■ Pamper the volunteer seedlings for a few weeks with extra water and protect them from slugs. Fertilize gently when they've grown about two inches tall. Now you can enjoy a garden of annuals that comes back perennially.

Geraniums can make it through a mild winter, if you remember to move them to a frost-free storage area. Water them very little during the winter to encourage dormancy. Wait until spring, when you see signs of new growth. Then chop off the top of the old geranium, remove any buds that are forming, and wait for a new plant to spring from the old stump. You may not get any flowers until midsummer, but you won't get geraniums any cheaper than the ones you winter over yourself.

Most-Asked Annual Growing Questions

Q. *I would love to have more flowers in my garden, but during the summer we go away for weeks at a time, and there is no one around to water and weed a flower garden. What can we plant that would survive our vacations?*
A. Wildflowers and native plants to the rescue. Nobody waters the lilies of the field, and they look splendid enough. Forget-me-nots, violets, and daisies are wonderful wildflowers that have been domesticated by plant breeders, but are still tough enough to survive in a yard with an absent owner.

If you need a more formal flower, plant geraniums. Water them well just before you leave and then cover with a mulch of bark chips to seal in the moisture.

If you live in an area where the summers are hot, plant drought-resistant annuals like nasturtiums and portulaca. You can be nasty to a nasturtium and treat a portulaca poorly — your reward will be bright blooms all summer long. These two sun-loving annuals will grow in lousy soil and tolerate weeks of drought. The only thing they demand is sunshine.

Q. *Is it better to buy flower seeds from a local store or are easier-to-grow flowers found in seed catalogues?*
A. Do both. Your local garden center may have a better selection of regional favorites, but ordering from a seed catalogue has advantages, too. Even if you're a lazy gardener, force yourself to send for at least one free seed catalogue. The color pictures and growing hints are well worth the price of a stamp, and, since catalogues arrive in your mailbox during the winter off-season, you'll have plenty

of time to browse through their pages for extra information and inspiration. If you do indulge in some mail-order flower power, keep your wits about you and your impulses under control. Easy-to-grow is the phrase lazy gardeners look for before they succumb to the lure of beautiful pictures.

Q. *I thought marigolds were supposed to be easy to grow, but my little transplants are dying. I brought them home a few weeks ago, planted them carefully and have been watering every day. The bottom leaves turned brown first and now the deathly look is climbing upward on the stem of the plant. Am I responsible for these marigold murders?*

A. You may be guilty of drowning your marigolds with too much attention. The clue to this mysterious malady is that you watered your marigolds every day. Unless you planted in very sandy soil and had exceptionally hot weather, you shouldn't have to water a bed of flowers that often. Marigolds need soil that drains well, or they'll quickly develop root rot and the oldest (and lowest) leaves curl up and die. Let the soil become slightly dry to the touch before watering your marigolds, and grow them in a sunny spot.

Q. *Help! There is soft white fur growing on the leaves of my zinnias! The foliage starts to look blotchy and then sprouts forth with this white growth. What is going on?*

A. That coat of downy white fur is downy mildew growing on your plants. Zinnias are great for hot, dry climates, but if you try to grow them when the weather is cool or in a spot where the plants don't get good air circulation, mildew moves in. Fungal diseases like mildew are sometimes controlled with fungicidal sprays, but the lazy way out of this mess is to remove every other plant in your bed of zinnias and see if the extra elbow room encourages healthier plants. Root out and throw away your infected zinnias if the mildew keeps coming on strong.

Q. *Bugs are flocking to my nasturtiums. Tiny black insects are stuck to the stems and undersides of the nasturtium leaves. What should I spray them with?*

A. Try soapy water or a strong jet of water. Those herds of insects are aphids, and they can be squished with your fingers, hosed off the plants, or killed with an insecticidal soap. Nasturtiums attract aphids from miles around, but this doesn't have to be a reason to ban them from your garden. I've seen nasturtium plants with a heavy helping of aphids grazing on their leaves, and a healthy dose of flowers blooming in spite of it. Grow your nasturtiums off by themselves in an out-of-the-way corner that you never get around to watering. Now consider the nasturtiums sacrificial flowers that will lure the aphids away from your other, more fragile plants.

CHAPTER SEVEN

Perennials: Many Happy Returns on Your Energy Investment

There are thousands of different perennial plants that flower year after year. No matter what type of soil you have, or how nasty your weather is, you can always find certain perennials that will thrive and bloom. Your biggest problem will be narrowing down your choices.

Flowers that grow from bulbs are considered perennials because they come back every year. Bulbs were already discussed in Chapter Four, so we'll concentrate on the other types of perennial plants.

If you're a speed reader, get ready to put on the brakes. Deciding what kinds of plants to label as perennials can be a bit confusing. Many perennials have swollen roots much like a bulb. These roots may be called *tubers* or *rhizomes*. Sometimes these roots will be referred to as bulbs when you order them from a nursery or garden catalogue. To add to the perennial confusion is the fact that some perennials take two years before they reach blooming size and so are called *biannuals*. Other plants, like the geranium, are annuals in some climates but are considered perennials in warmer climates because they can survive the winter.

There are many perennials without specialized roots that are easy to grow from seed, and perennial plants that rarely flower but are sold alongside the other flowering perennials because of their lovely foliage.

Just goes to show that botanists may have the classifying power, but Mother Nature still controls the flower.

Lazy gardeners don't have to worry about all this classifying chaos. They can just concentrate on finding flowers that will bloom without fuss and return without replanting.

If what you want is a blooming plant with impressive flowers and a forgiving personality, then let me introduce you to the three favorite perennial flowers of the lazy gardener. There may be other flowers that grow with less work, but no other perennials are as easy to find for sale and perform so well in so many different gardens across the country. These three perennials even have a nostalgic appeal. They're relatives of the very same plants that everyone's grandmother grew a generation ago.

The Triplets of Delight: Irises, Daylilies, and Peonies

Irises: There is Siberian iris for wet spots, and bearded iris for well-drained spots, and even Japanese iris. Members of this floral family all have swordlike foliage and complex flowers that remind me of a dragon's jaws. Irises will bloom for years around an abandoned house and survive winter storms, summer drought, and a yard full of active children. Try to dig up your extra irises and throw them away, and they'll even sprout up and bloom next to your garbage can. The bearded iris is the most popular type and the most tolerant of lousy soil. Add an iris clump to the corner of your yard and watch it increase in size each year. The grasslike foliage that remains after the blooms makes a great background for other flowering plants. If you have a clump of iris that stops blooming, you may have to dig it up, divide it, and improve the soil before you replant it. Division and multiplication of perennials will be covered later in this chapter. Don't worry too much about pleasing this perennial. Iris is easy to ignore.

Daylilies: I really love plants that are difficult to kill, and daylilies bloom through the meanest of murder attempts. They don't even need decent soil, although they'll certainly bloom better if you add a little compost or steer manure to their planting hole.

Daylilies sprout forth from grassy clumps of foliage, and they bloom in the summer months when you are outdoors most often.

If your garden is much too prissy for the casual sprawl of a traditional daylily border, investigate the new tetraploid daylilies. These exotic-looking plants have fewer leaves and more flowers, but still inherit the easy-going attitude that daylilies are famous for.

If you grow weary of tending a vegetable plot, plant the whole thing in daylilies and then dine on the blossoms all summer long. The Chinese use daylilies in many of their recipes, and since the flowers last for only a day, you won't feel like you're robbing your garden of color by grazing rather than gazing on your daylilies.

Peonies: This is a fancy-looking flower for someone with no time to garden. Peonies open full, fat, and fragrant as a rose and sport very lush and attractive foliage. Here is one perennial that won't mind if you never get around to dividing it. As long as you don't plant the tubers too deep (no more than two inches of soil should cover the tops), your peonies will bloom in almost any soil and tolerate hot summers and cold winters. Peonies bloom in late spring, but the foliage stays neat, compact, and green all summer long.

Peonies must have been popular with the founders of Enumclaw, Washington, the small town where we live. Virtually every historical home sprouts forth with the same variety of dark pink peony blooms in May. It's obvious to me where all these gigantic peony clumps came from. There's a mansion right on Main Street that is enclosed by a long thick hedge of peony plants. I'm sure that, years ago, there was a high-society gathering at this mansion and all the guests were given starts from the newly planted peony hedge as they left the party. Everybody must have gone straight home and planted the pioneer peony tubers in a shallow grave. The owners of these grand old homes may have changed over the years, but the living legacy of the pink peonies lives on in Enumclaw. Plant peonies for permanence — they'll probably outlive you.

Other Forgiving Perennials: There were once wildflowers and native plants that grew on the very spot that you now call your garden. These original plants may be the ancestors of the modern-day perennials that you can buy today. Do a little research to determine which perennials are best suited for your laid-back gardening style. If you live where the summers are hot and dry, then perennials like coreopsis and Rudbeckia daisies will feel right at home. If you enjoy a mild climate like that of the Pacific Northwest, then the foxgloves, bleeding heart, and hardy geraniums will do well in both their native form and as the more showy varieties that the plant breeders have developed. On the eastern seaboard, phlox, lilies, and blooming rock garden plants like penstemon thrive as easily as their ancestors did.

When choosing perennials for your team of garden bloomers, the object of the game is to match up what you have in the way of sun, soil, and moisture with the needs of one of the flowering perennials. In other words, if you live in the middle of a rain forest, don't fill your yard with sun-loving perennials like chrysanthemums. The people to poll for local flowering favorites are your neighbors and the owners of your local nurseries. Beauty is important, but don't let your heart have the final word. Dahlias may be dazzling, but unless you intend to make a serious staking, feeding, and watering commitment, plus protect such a tender plant from the winter cold, you had better stick to growing daylilies.

Easy-to-Grow Perennials for the Sun

Coreopsis: Yellow flowers and a sunny disposition make this a cheerful plant that will flower all summer. No pests will invade this plant, and all you really have to do is pick the flowers. Compact plants that look great when massed together.

Creeping Phlox: So low and compact, it makes a great groundcover. The tiny pink or white spring flowers will completely cover the foliage. Phlox is fine for rock gardens and slopes, or to fill in any sunny, dry spots amongst the shrubs. This plant actually likes lousy, rocky soil. Not a good choice for cool, moist gardens, but very drought-tolerant.

Dianthus, or Pinks: Not only does this little charmer have spiky blue-gray foliage, but the carnation-like blossoms are fragrant as well. Another perennial for around rocks or walls, but try to grow some near a doorway so you can enjoy the fragrance and fill your vases with the pink flowers. Newer varieties come in white and red. Dianthus likes gritty soil with a little lime thrown in.

Shasta Daisy: Make sure you grow only the dwarfs when picking out members of the daisy or chrysanthemum family. Lazy gardeners have no time for staking up plants. The dwarf Shasta daisy has large white flowers and blooms again and again. This hardy plant makes a big splash without a lot of maintenance.

Candytuft, or Iberis: The nickname for this white-blooming rockery flower is century plant. They may not live for a full century, but there are gnarled masses of candytuft cascading over rock walls that have outlived the houses they were planted near to beautify. Candytuft will bloom in light shade or full sun and it isn't picky about the soil. The foliage is evergreen and can look quite tidy if kept trimmed. I have seen low borders of candytuft pruned into a formal hedge shape that looked a lot like boxwood.

I recommend this plant to anyone who works the swing shift or enjoys an active night life. Coming home at midnight when the candytuft is blooming is an eye-widening delight. The white flowers seem to glow iridescently in the dark.

Sweet William: Just an old-fashioned flower, but one my grandmother grew for years in the worst soil. The variety she had bloomed red with a lacy white edging. She donated a clump to me for our new gardens, but I accepted the gift before we were ready to plant anything. All I did was stick the poor plant into a hole in the ground while we spent the summer building our house. No water, no fertilizing— just a semi-shaded spot in the dirt. It bloomed anyway. It always does.

About the only problem with sweet William is finding someone who sells it. This perennial is given away so readily by generous gardeners that many local growers don't bother to carry it. Check the Source Guide on page 161 and order sweet William from a perennial specialist if you can't find a nursery that sells it.

Easy-to-Grow Perennials for the Shade

Primrose: If you have overhead shade and a woodsy soil, you can tiptoe down a primrose path with the greatest of ease. Don't try growing this woodland favorite if your soil is dry or sandy.

There is a low-growing, deep violet primrose called "Wanda" that charms the heart of every gardener lucky enough to discover it. Primroses bloom early in the spring, and Wanda is one of the first to bloom, surviving wet winters and dry summers and even resisting attacks from slugs.

Give primroses plenty of water in the summer and they may thank you with a bonus set of blooms in the fall. A wonderful perennial to plant amongst your spring-flowering bulbs.

Hosta: These shade lovers seem to be the newest darling of serious and committed gardeners. Actually, hosta was a lazy-gardening favorite years before it was discovered by the "it hasta be hosta" set.

The leaves are long, large, and tropical-looking and come in cool shades of green and white or rippling blues. Plant hosta on the north or east side of the house, where it's cool and dark. Then just enjoy.

Lily-of-the-Valley: Plant a few of these plants under the shade of a tree, and they'll probably be blooming for your grandchildren to pick. They do need organic matter in the soil (add peat moss), and you will have to water during droughts. Lily-of-the-valley will carpet the ground with fragrant bell-shaped flowers, but only if it likes your soil. Give up and plant something else if this plant fails to flourish after a year or two.

Coral Bells: Tall, dainty stems rise above the low-growing foliage and bloom as airy as baby's breath. I use coral bells to edge every pathway and to soften the borders of the walkways. The knee-high blooms dance in the breeze but never need staking. The plants have shallow roots and transplant with ease, so you can spread them all over the garden. This perennial will tolerate sun as long as it gets plenty of water, and it never needs fertilizing.

Where to Get Perennials

The triple delight perennials (irises, daylilies, and peonies) are sold at many garden centers in the fall and spring alongside the spring bulb displays. They all come in a wide range of colors, so good luck trying to make up your mind.

Perennials may also be ordered from seed and nursery mail-order companies. The photographs and cultural information in these catalogues make them the best gardening bargain around. Even if you never place an order, a perennial plant catalogue makes a great encyclopedia. Get on some mailing lists and soak up the free information. Reading is one chore that lazy gardeners can do from their easy chairs.

Just remember that you will have to nurse the new plants for the first year after the transplant, so don't take on too many patients at once. Another caution is not to be swayed by the appealing photos and order the prettiest flower on the page. A beginner with a yen for perennial plants should look for the words "easy to grow" first and stay away from expensive rarities.

Another way to get perennial plants that will thrive on neglect is to liberate them from a renegade garden. Look for houses scheduled for demolition or places with an unkempt lawn and boarded-up windows. Get the owner's permission (City Hall can tell you who owns title to any house in town) and then dig up the blooming plants that deserve a new "leaf on life." Except for trading plants with fellow gardeners, nothing is more rewarding than adopting an orphan plant and enjoying the petals of gratitude that shower you for years. One garden's discards are another garden's delights.

Growing Tips for Perennial Happiness

■ Improve the soil before you plant, then continue with a mulch every fall. You can sprinkle a granular or liquid fertilizer around your perennial plants if you feel generous and energetic one year, but if you improve your soil adding fertilizer won't be necessary. The more you work on the soil, the less you'll have to work on your plants.

■ Water deeply during summer droughts. A leaky hose laid throughout the bed is an efficient way to water. Cover that hose with a thick mulch of bark or compost and you'll not only hide the hose, but conserve water, too.

■ Plant in drifts or ribbonlike waves of plants, not in square or rectangular planting patterns. Mother Nature has a preference for curves. It was humans who designed the first checkerboard.

■ Just because you're lazy, it doesn't mean you have to be boring and predictable. Add at least one new plant every year, so that you're continually trying different flowers. That way you won't feel so bad when something dies. Tell yourself that the weaker plants just have to fade away to make room for the newcomers you need to test.

■ Allow yourself to fall in love with a favorite perennial. Remember that work turns into hobby when you dote on a plant that enraptures you. I nominate Asiatic lilies as a perennial that takes a little more effort to grow, but is definitely worth the fuss. The gigantic blooms slightly resemble the wild tiger lilies from which they were derived. Not to be confused with the common daylily, Asiatic lilies are regal and expensive-looking. They add class to even a laid-back landscape.

■ Perennials need to be divided up every so often (see instructions on page 115), but, if the plant is doing well and producing flowers, why risk working up a sweat? Divide your perennials when they show a shortage of blooms or otherwise act like they need it. For some plants, this could be every other year; for others, never.

■ If your climate is hot and dry, then plant your flowering plants close together, so they can shade the soil for each other. If you garden where summers can be cool and moist, space your plants farther apart than recommended to increase air circulation and cut down on mildew and fungal disease.

■ Add a focal point to dramatize the flower grouping in your yard. A sundial or birdbath surrounded by your flower collection changes that simple flower bed into an impressive-looking garden destination. Make sure you can view the scene from indoors for even more enjoyment.

■ Leave room for a little path in the back of the bed, or add stepping stones through the middle. You will need to get up close to your flowers in order to clip off spent blooms and inspect for bugs. There's no reason you can't be up-front about it. An obvious pathway will encourage others to get a noseful of floral scents.

Where and When to Plug in a Perennial Plant

■ Attack plants while they sleep. This means you should wait until your perennial plants are dormant in early spring or early autumn before you move them about or add them to the garden. Mail-order companies will send out your plants at the correct planting time, and garden centers will display perennial tubers and potted plants at their proper planting times. Early spring is the time to visit nurseries, if you want already-started perennial plants.

■ Put in a low-growing perennial around your garden accents. Creeping thyme or dwarf iris blooming around the base of a birdbath gives the garden feature a more stable, tied-to-the-ground look.

■ Give spreading perennials a home where they can roam. You won't have to divide them quite so often if you can afford to let them spread. Plant annuals around young perennials while you wait for them to mature and fill in.

■ If you have flowering shrubs growing along your property line, plug in a couple of perennial plants to extend the blooming season. Summer bloomers like daylilies and daisies would work especially well, since most blooming shrubs flower in the spring.

Summer Care of Your Flower Garden

■ Water and weed all summer long. A deep watering once a week is all that most perennial flowers require. Put down a thick mulch and you can skip the weeding.

■ No bugs should be allowed to take over the flowers, but a few chewed leaves is no reason to panic. A healthy plant can resist most insects, so keep the plants watered. Use soapy water to wash away aphids and spider mites. You'll find more pest-fighting tips in Chapter Ten.

■ Keep the dead flowers from going to seed and you'll get more blooms. Dead-heading also keeps the plant tidy.

■ If disease invades the flower bed, remove the worst plants to give better air circulation. Don't overwater and stop fertilizing any sickly plant.

Fall Care of the Flower Bed

■ Don't be so quick to cut back perennial plants that have been damaged by the frost. Those ugly frozen plant skeletons help protect the roots from winter freezes.

■ Don't dose up your flower garden with chemical fertilizers in the fall. You may encourage a quick growth spurt that will be killed off by the frost.

■ If you live where winters are severe, then fall is the time to pile rotted leaves and compost around your perennials. Not only will this blanket of garden garbage protect the plants, but the winter rains will wash the nutrients down into the soil just in time for the spring growth spurt.

Spring Care of the Flower Bed

■ As soon as you notice new growth in the garden, that's your signal to pull back the mulch from around the base of your plants. A heavy blanket of mulch may keep the soil from warming up in the spring.

■ As you remove the mulch, look for slugs and bugs that have overwintered, and then stab, squash, and pulverize the enemy with your garden trowel. Not only will your quest for revenge be fulfilled, but this early spring bug battering reduces the population by wiping out the enemy before mating season.

■ Late spring is the best time to fertilize your perennial flower bed. Now, don't panic if you can't find the time or energy. Remember that all lazy-gardening flowers still bloom if you don't feed. I usually scatter a granular plant food amongst the plants without measuring. This is called broadcasting the product, but it takes a little practice to make sure you don't broadcast an overdose on some poor plant. Better to sprinkle too little fertilizer than too much.

■ If broadcasting fertilizer as you tiptoe through your flower beds makes you feel a bit like a spring fairy, you can use a liquid plant food instead. Fish fertilizer or an all-purpose plant food that dissolves in water is easier for some gardeners to apply.

Winter Care of Flower Beds

■ Thumb through plant and seed catalogues for inspiration.

■ Daydream about your beautiful blooming flowerbeds.

■ Devote lots of time to storing up energy by taking it easy in the winter. Practice relaxing in front of a fireplace.

Multiplying and Dividing Your Perennials

Many perennials appreciate getting cut up every couple of years. This keeps them in blooming good condition. Experts recommended that you perform this operation in early spring or early fall. The shock of the division can then be performed while the plants are under the "anesthetic" of cold-weather dormancy. I want to declare right here and now that I have divided perennials, added perennials, multiplied perennials, and subtracted perennials in winter, spring, summer, and fall and have always had wonderful luck. It may be easier on the plant if you divide while dormant, but you won't be branded a ruthless plant murderer if you divide something up during the summer months.

This means you should go ahead and move your plants when you sell the house, even if the gardening books tell you it's the wrong time of year. Give your visiting sister a piece of peony if she asks for it in August. Luckily for you, plants pay no attention to what the gardening books say. You should only be growing the hard-to-kill perennials anyway, so lighten up. You're the boss.

The dividing process is not as difficult as the name implies. Even if you had trouble with long division in grade school, you can pass plant division with blooming colors. Just read through the steps below and, remember, it's pretty hard to kill the recommended, easy-growing perennials, even if you take an ax to them.

■ First, water the perennial deeply. Moist soil will cling better to the roots.

■ Next, whack off the top half of the plant if it has leaves that are tall and overgrown. This is usually the case if you're dividing plants in early fall. That way you can see what you're up against.

■ Try to insert a pitchfork or hand rake into the clump and pull away outer sections of the plant. If you're not getting roots with the sections you pull apart, give up and go on to the next step.

■ For really tough or tuberous plants, you will need to lift up the entire clump and then use a sharp knife or axe to separate the side plants from the mother.

■ This will sound cruel, but you can throw away the old mother plant if there are plenty of healthy babies to replace her with. The inner core of large perennial clumps is overly mature and on the decline. You want to replant the vigorous new growth on the outer perimeter of the clump.

■ Replant the divided sections into holes with improved soil. Do not make the mortal sin of planting your perennials too deep. Firm the soil around the plants and then water them in. That's it. No need to fertilize right after you divide a plant. Water it often instead.

Most gardeners end up with more perennial plants then they can find room for. Don't stop dividing your crowded perennials just because you've run out of yard. Just bring some moist newspaper out to the garden when you decide it's dividing day. Roll the extra plants into the soggy newspaper and stuff them all into a plastic bag. Now you've got three or four days to find a doorstep to dump them on. Think of people with new homes, or community plant sales, or offer your easy-growing perennials to fellow lazy gardeners. If you can visualize someone looking forward to your extras, it makes it easier to go out there and get the job done. The lazy gardener needs every bit of incentive to go motivated into taking action.

You've probably heard of Johnny Appleseed, but there's room in the history books for a modern-day perennial planter. Take your perennial divisions and tuck them into the soil around roadsides or parking strips, or add them to the evergreen and ever-boring landscapes put in by government agencies. There's a good chance those iris tubers or daylily divisions will take root and bloom into a colorful surprise for years to come. There must be some sort of special blessing for all the good souls who leave this earth a little more beautiful than they found it. Go forth and beautify— even lazy gardeners can plant perennial flowers and have time left over for playful pursuits.

Most-Asked Perennial Growing Questions

Q. *We moved into an old house, and there are great clumps of perennial flowers planted about. I want to plant all the flowers together somehow, instead of having them so close to the house. How do I organize such a garden when I don't know the names of most of these plants?*

A. It isn't necessary to be formally introduced to the plants in your garden. You can become great friends just by taking the time to observe where the plant is growing now and how that compares to where you want to move it. If you have a mystery plant, wait until it's done blooming and then transplant it to its new home. That way, you'll know its growth habit and it will be easy to arrange the tall plants in the back of the bed and the shorter perennials in the front. You can find proper names for all your mystery plants by either thumbing through a plant catalogue or taking a sample of flower and foliage to a garden club or nursery. But if the plant grows well, there's no need to research its background— just name it yourself and stop worrying about nomenclature. The common names of many plants vary from region to region because of all the clever and descriptive names their owners have given them.

Q. *Some of the perennial plants in my rockery are so old and huge that they're ugly. Can I divide these giant clumps?*
A. Not all perennial plants can be easily pulled apart and divided. Most rockery plants with fibrous root systems are better off rejuvenated by stem cuttings. This means you pull apart sections of the plant in early spring and root the young outermost pieces in moist sand or a glass of water. Of course, this may seem like too much work for a lazy gardener, so go ahead and stick the little pieces of plant you pull off into the moist soil of your rockery. Use a smooth stone to hold the stem cutting in place. With a little luck a few of these casual cuttings may take hold.

Q. *I sent for some peony tubers a couple of years ago, and, although the plant sprouts forth healthy-looking leaves every summer, it has never bloomed. How can I get my stingy peony to produce flowers?*
A. Time to fess up. Did you plant your peony too deep? The tuber should be just a few inches below the surface of the soil. Peonies also need at least half a day of sun. If you buried all chance of blooms, lift your pouting peony out and replant it at a lesser depth. Your peonies may also be a bit immature to handle flower production. It sometimes takes a couple of years for young tubers to grow to flowering size.

Q. *I love the big Shasta daisies that grow in my garden, but they always flop over onto the shorter flowers and make a sprawling mess. Can I prune them somehow to keep them compact?*
A. No. Tall perennial flowers cannot be sheared back and kept low the way some shrubs can. There are dwarf forms of the taller perennials, and lupines, phlox, and tidy knee-high daisies are among these newly developed compact plants. If you really need the height in your garden, then use wire tomato cages or a straightened coat hanger to hold up the fainting flowers in your bed. Tall perennials do well when planted next to a fence. Then you can corral the floppy stems by circling them with twine and tying the bundle to the fence slats.

Q. *I have a flower bed of perennial flowers, but it just never looks as full and colorful as I'd like it to. Most of the perennials that do well for me bloom in the spring, and my flower bed looks drab in the summer. I've tried summer-blooming perennials, but only the daylilies survived, and I want something that grows lower.*
A. All you have to do to fill out your flower garden is let the annual flowers fraternize with the perennials. Most annuals bloom all summer, and petunias, marigolds, and fibrous begonias are just a few of the easy-to-grow annuals that will stay low

to the ground. Add some large boulders to that garden of yours for color contrast and a smooth texture. Plant a few dwarf-blooming shrubs like potentilla if your summers are hot, or heather if your summers are cool. Don't let some arbitrary gardening guideline keep you from mixing all types of plants with your perennials. Plant your garden to please yourself.

CHAPTER EIGHT

Let Your Garden Go to Pots

Go ahead and admit it. There are millions of you out there, and it's nothing to be ashamed of. Even the easy-to-grow perennial and annual flowers are not easy enough for you to grow. Maybe it's all the bending and lifting that gardening in the ground requires. Perhaps it's just your black thumb, or a demanding career or active family life that keeps you from putting in flower beds. If a blooming border of flowers will not fit into your space or lifestyle, then relax and fess up to the truth. The only kind of gardening easy enough for some people is puttering in pots.

Container gardening is perfect for the lazy gardener. There is practically no bending, weeding, or hoeing to worry about. You can take your gardens with you when you move or store them in the shade when you go on vacation. Container gardening allows you the freedom of putting flowers exactly where you want them, no matter what the soil is like. You don't even need a piece of ground. Hanging baskets make gardening in the sky a space-saving solution.

There is always a catch in the gardening game, and your container garden will need more passes with the watering can and require more fumbling around with fertilizers than if the same flowers were planted in the ground. There are some other growing concerns to consider before you let the yard go to pots. A good soil mix and a good plant mix are the winning combination that will score more flowers for a lot less fuss.

Potting Soil for Contented Container Gardens

You will need to use a special soil mix in all your pots. Don't make the mistake of using dirt right from your garden. The soil for pots should be lightweight and free from disease. It must drain quickly, yet retain plenty of moisture. Potting soils that you buy in plastic bags at garden centers will have special additives like perlite or vermiculite, which keep the soil from packing down and suffocating your potted plants. Garden centers also sell bags of white perlite and silvery brown vermiculite to thrifty gardeners who want to mix up their own potting soil.

Here's my potting soil recipe for the gardener who's more frugal than lazy.

Cooking up your own potting soil is a quick and easy job, one that gives every adult an excuse to play in the dirt.

1. Add one-third damp peat moss, one-third perlite or vermiculite, and one-third processed steer manure or compost.

2. Blend well with a hoe in a large wheelbarrow or on a tarp-covered surface. Season the mix with an all-purpose granular fertilizer, or sprinkle in a slow-release plant food like Osmocote. Use the amount recommended on the package.

3. Spoon the mixture into your pots and barrels and water well.

I like to let the " batter" stand for twenty-four hours or longer, then water it again to make sure the peat moss is thoroughly saturated. Warm water does a better job of wetting peat moss than cold water. You can tell when the soil mix is ready for planting when it retains enough moisture to feel damp, but not wet.

■ You don't have to replace all the soil in your pots every spring. Just scrape away the dead plants and remove the top three inches of potting soil. Then work in a fresh layer of potting soil before adding the new plants.

Bigger Pots, Smaller Demands

Flowers in small pots, clay pots, and crowded pots need more water and fertilizer then container gardens planted in large tubs. It is easier to tend three large barrels of blooms than to care for six smaller pots holding the same number of flowers.

■ If you have very large pots and plants like annuals with shallow roots, fill up the bottom half of the pots with Styrofoam pellets, or "peanuts." (Our kids call these chunks of packing foam "ghost poo.") A layer of this artificial spirit manure allows for good drainage, but is also lightweight and a good insulator. As long as you give your flowering plants at least ten inches of soil to sink their roots into, you can substitute drainage material for expensive potting soil in the bottom half of any large pot.

Best Pot Spots

■ Set your pots on a bed of gravel or bricks, bordering a drive or walkway. Now you won't have to worry about stepping all over the plants if you need more room. Putting a gravel or paved surface next to a walkway or drive gives the user a more comfortable sense of space.

■ Pot up some welcoming plants near the front door, right below the doorbell. Now you can let the rest of the yard go to weed, and your visitors will never notice.

Anyone that calls at the door will be so dazzled by the porch flowers that they won't even notice the overgrown lawn or laid-back landscape maintenance.

■ Set some pots underneath trees or hang them from overhead branches. Impatiens and lobelia welcome these shady lanes.

■ Hang a pot outside the kitchen window, so the blooming plant can be viewed from both inside and outside. This little inspiration can make washing dishes less of a pain, and you'll remember to recycle the dirty dishwater if there are thirsty flowers right outside the window.

■ Festoon a wall or the blank side of a house with flowers. Any bare wall can be transformed into a hanging garden with pot brackets to engage the containers and flowers to engage the beholder.

■ Keep containers close to you. Wherever you sit to relax and enjoy the garden is the perfect place to put a pot.

The Laziest Way to Water

I've said it before, but it bears repeating. A well-planned irrigation system conserves the most labor and the most water. A watering system for potted plants can be simply devised with plastic tubing that carries water to each pot. Hardware stores are often a better supply source for this type of "spaghetti" tubing than nurseries and garden centers. The plastic tubing can even be pinned up the wall and then dropped over hanging baskets to discreetly water your suspended pots. Just turn on the faucet, and all your potted plants will be watered at once.

For just a few pots of flowers, invest in an easy-to-handle watering can. Park the watering can next to your pots, so that every time you see the flowers you'll be reminded that they may be thirsty.

Food and the Potted Flower

Every potted plant would like you to get one thing straight. They need to be fed. Plants that are growing in the ground may still bloom and grow if you don't get around to fertilizing. There are nutrients in the soil that can support plant life, and the soil is replenished each year when an organic mulch is added in the fall. This is not true for plants growing in pots! The root systems of potted plants are trapped with a tiny source of soil, and they can't go searching the area for more nutrients. Add to that fact that most potting soils are made up of lightweight materials like perlite and peat moss that have little or no nutritional value. Your potted plants could starve to death if you don't fertilize them. The more flowers you want, the more fertilizing you should do. Of course, if you fertilize too much, your plants will show tip burn and leaf scorch from taking in too much food too fast.

Here are two ways for the lazy gardener to fertilize without fear:

The One-Time Shot

Use a plant food that releases the nutrients very slowly all summer long. There is a slow-release fertilizer called Osmocote that is favored by professional growers. The fertilizer is encased in tiny beads that slowly leak nutrients into the soil whenever you water. Osmocote is sold at many nurseries and garden centers. There are also solid fertilizers that come in a stick or stake form. Once the fertilizer stake is inserted into moist soil, it begins to slowly dissolve, releasing nutrients for months. These slow-release fertilizer stakes are also available for using around trees and shrubs.

Slow-release plant foods are perfect for the forgetful gardener. Just remember to use them once, at the beginning of the season, and you can forget about fertilizing after that.

Other Meal Plans

If you already use a watering can to keep your flowers moist, then it won't take much extra effort to spoon in a water-soluble fertilizer. Plant foods that dissolve in water are inexpensive and effective and you don't even have to stir them up to get them to dissolve. Instead, you can just get into the habit of adding the fertilizer first and then filling the can with water. I put my thumb over the hose opening, so that a forceful jet of water will stir up the fertilizer and dissolve it completely by the time the watering can is filled.

No matter how lazy you feel, read and follow the label directions before you measure out the fertilizer for the first time. Pull up a chair and take your time. If there is no measuring scoop included with the fertilizer, tie an old spoon to the watering can or use the lid to measure. Remember to use a little less than recommended, never more.

Granular fertilizers are the type you mix right into the soil at planting time or sprinkle on top of the soil and then wash into the root zone by watering. They don't act as quickly as the fertilizers you mix with water, but you don't need to use them as often. Granular fertilizers are convenient to use if you can mix them into the potting soil before the plants are added.

Potted Plants without the Pots

Here's a way to pot up some color without buying a pot. Just use the plastic bag your potting soil came in to plant up a pillow of blooms. Lay the bag on its side; poke holes in the bottom for drainage and holes in the top to insert the plants. If you use creeping plants like petunias, the flowers will soon cover and shade the plastic bag, and you'll have a pillow of flowers. These "pillows" can even be set right into your flower beds for easy color you only dreamed about before.

If you have a good source of sphagnum moss or tree moss, you can line baskets and wire frames with moss instead of plastic, then fill in the cavity with soil and plants. Moss baskets are cool- and natural-looking, perfect for hanging in a shady spot. Just because you don't want to work hard, it doesn't mean you can't be creative and original. Plastic pots are not required for container gardening.

Barrels of Blooms

Recycled whiskey barrels make wonderful places to grow flowers. The half barrels are inexpensive, yet big enough to grow roses and dwarf fruit trees and still provide enough space for an edging of cascading flowers. Here's how to help your barrels blossom better:

■ Fill the bottom half of the barrel with Styrofoam chunks or gravel, if all you'll be growing are shallow-rooted annuals. You will need at least a two-inch layer of drainage material, no matter what you want to grow.

■ If the rustic look of the barrel doesn't appeal to you, but the price and size does, you can paint the barrels with outdoor deck paint or build a bottomless box around the tub with any type of siding.

■ Filling up a whole barrel with flowers every spring can be overwhelming, so plant an evergreen shrub in the center of the whiskey barrel and then add spring-blooming bulbs and summer-blooming annuals around the edges for seasonal color. Dwarf Alberta spruce looks like a mini Christmas tree and doesn't mind being confined to a pot for years. Hino crimson azaleas and dwarf rhododendrons have compact roots that adjust well to life in a barrel, as long as you keep them well watered. Choose tiny bulbs that will re-

Easiest-to-Grow Flowers for Pots of Spring Color

PRIMROSES   DWARF DAFFODIL BULBS
PANSIES   SNOWDROP BULBS
CROCUS BULBS   SHORT-STEMMED TULIPS

Easiest-to-Grow Flowers for Pots of Summer Color

For Sun:	For Shade:
LOBELIA	GERANIUMS
MARIGOLDS	IMPATIENS
BEGONIAS	SALVIA
ALYSSUM	COLEUS
	NASTURTIUMS

Easiest-to-Grow Evergreen Shrubs for Containers

RHODODENDRONS   JAPANESE HOLLY
BOXWOOD   JUNIPERS
DWARF ALBERTA SPRUCE

turn every spring, such as snowdrops and crocuses for the inner border of the pot. For summer color you can add spreading annuals like lobelia and alyssum for around the outer edges. Creeping and draping annuals will help hide the dying foliage from the spring bulbs.

Most-Asked Questions about Container Gardening

Q. *I love the look of clay pots, but they always seem to crack and break after a year or two. I like to use very large pots, so don't tell me to store them indoors for the winter.*
A. I know you don't want to hear this, but if you live where it freezes in the winter, then indoor storage is the only fail-safe way to protect your clay pots from cracking. You can do a lot to reduce fractures in the clay by sealing both the inside and outside of your new clay pots with a water-proofing shellac. Buy this type of sealant where paints are sold. It will give your pots a shiny gloss and prevent the clay from absorbing moisture, which then freezes and thaws, weakening the pot.

You must also realize that all clay pots were not created equal. The terra cotta of Mexico is softer and cracks more easily than the clays from Italy. Some American-made pots are gaining a reputation for exceptional crack resistance. Lazy gardeners only want to buy their pots once.

Q. *What can I do about the stains that my container gardens leave on the deck and patio? I tried moving the pots about all summer to reduce the chance of staining, but what I got instead of one dark stain was lots of lighter stains.*
A. Moving your pots around all summer is a dreadful solution to a simple problem. Instead, just leave the pots in one place full time. Who's going to see the stain if the pot never gets moved? You could also consider using wall brackets and overhead hanging pots to give you more room and fewer stains on your surface. Instead of plastic saucers under your patio pots, use thick pieces of cork to insulate the moisture from the wood and cement below.

Q. *I like to buy my container gardens already planted-up from a local nursery. I notice that these mixed planters include both sun-loving and shade-loving flowers. Why do nurseries do this, and where should I set a pot that needs both sun and shade?*
A. Grow your mixed planter in a sunny spot. Shade-tolerant plants will thrive in the sunshine better than sun-loving flowers will survive in the shade. It's perfectly proper to put "shady" plants in with sun-seeking flowers because, although we think of lobelia, impatiens, and begonias as flowers that need the shade, they will bloom happily in the sunshine, as long as they get plenty of water and the spot is sun-filled but not heat-drenched. Very hot spots against west- or south-facing walls are the killers.

Q. *Please tell me what flowers I can plant in my patio containers that won't need*

replacing every year. I am tired of buying new geraniums and marigolds every spring.
A. The ultimate in lazy gardening—perennials for your pots. Mix some spring-blooming bulbs with summer-blooming perennials and you can have a few years of color before the plants grow too crowded. Try the small tetraploid daylilies along with dwarf daffodils and rock-garden tulips.

Another solution to your growing problem is to pot up a good-natured rose bush. There are plenty of easy-to-grow floribunda and miniature roses that do well in containers.

Don't forget about the blooming evergreen shrubs that will adapt to a life of confinement. Flowering camellias, rhododendrons, and blooming potentilla are a few of the shrubs that can live for years in a pot.

CHAPTER NINE

No Naked Soil: Groundcovers and Mulches

It's time to return to morality and modesty in the garden. Bare-naked ground is not natural. Man may have been born fully exposed, but Mother Nature never meant for the soil to be nude, without so much as a fig leaf for cover.

If you've ever considered the lilies of the field, magnificent in their natural splendor, than you should also take note of the ground those lilies sink their roots into. From fields to forests, the soil is always properly dressed with a covering of leaves, grass, and debris that completely covers the soft soil below. Even if wind or a digging animal accidently exposes the soil, Mother Nature moves quickly to cover the naked earth again with sprouting plants and falling foliage.

Naked soil should not be allowed in the yards of lazy gardeners. Mother Nature knows best, and she insists on either plant life or a mulch for maximum modesty. Lazy gardeners must insist on soil coverage, too, and make use of either groundcover plants or a mulch.

Mulch — Like Frosting on the Cake

You can think of mulch as the perfect frosting for a wonderfully prepared bed of soil. A good organic mulch sits on top of the soil, gradually decaying and releasing nutrients. Rain takes these vitamins down to the root zone, where they feed your hungry plants. This is the way nature intended for plants to be fed.

By definition, a mulch is simply any material that can be spread on top of the soil. An organic mulch is made from material that decays over time. An inorganic mulch is a material like rocks or black plastic that doesn't break down in the soil.

An organic mulch does much more than just add natural fertilizers to your soil. Lazy gardeners should worship mulch as the answer to their maintenance prayers. Here are some of the other free services that a mulch provides:

■ Mulching traps moisture in the soil. The more you mulch, the less you have to water.

■ A thick mulch will smother weeds that come from below, and form a barrier to wind-borne weed seeds that come from above. The more you mulch, the less you have to weed.

■ A loose mulch will keep your soil from compacting. When the soil stays loose and friable, it transports oxygen better and grows healthier plants. The more you mulch, the less you have to hoe or cultivate.

■ Mulches keep your flowers clean. Rain splashing on naked soil will spatter mud and grit all over your fragile flowers.

■ A cushion of mulch softens the fall of fruit and berries. Splattered berries and bruised fruit attract rodents and wasps to the garden.

■ A mulch keeps your soil warmer during the winter and cooler during the summer. It's nature's natural insulator.

Types of Organic Mulches

Bark Chips: These are pieces of tree bark, often sold packaged in plastic bags at garden centers. Bark chips are also called bark dust when the pieces of bark are small and fine. Bark is one of the most attractive soil frostings you can spread. The bigger the chunks of bark, the more weed control it offers and the longer this mulch will last. The fine bark dust may need to be replenished more often because it decomposes easily, but if a mulch rots quickly, it also means it's improving your soil faster. As a general rule, if your soil needs improving, mulch with fine bark; if weeds are a problem, use the big chunks of bark.

Sawdust: Closely related to bark chips are wood chips and sawdust. Sawdust is like bark dust, in that it will decompose quickly to improve the soil, but a layer of sawdust robs nitrogen from the soil and may turn the plants pale and yellow. Just sprinkle bonemeal or a fertilizer high in nitrogen around the plants every time you add fresh sawdust as a mulch.

Pine Needles: Easy to spread and a fine weed block, pine needles are free for the taking in many parts of the country. They tend to make the soil acidic, so rhododendrons and azaleas particularly enjoy them as a mulch.

Cedar Shavings: A perfectly wonderful mulch if you're lucky enough to live near a source of cedar. The color and scent of cedar shavings are a natural in the garden, and cedar will also repel fleas and sprouting weeds. Unlike bark chips, cedar shavings won't push splinters into bare hands and feet, nor do they attract wood ants or termites. Like many other mulches, cedar shavings come in several forms.

I'd like to announce here and now that cedar is the mulch we use in our own backyard—and front yard too. We use the small curly shavings around our shrubs and the larger chunks, called cedar chips, in pathways and as a heavy weed block beneath trees.

We switched from using bark chips to cedar shavings several years ago, despite the rumors that cedar was bad for plants. It was whispered among gardeners that cedar gave off fumes that would stunt plant growth. Thank goodness the trees, flowers, and shrubs in our yard never heard these nasty lies. They grow and bloom just fine surrounded by cedar mulch and cedar shavings. The smell is clean, and the price is right.

There is only one sad side to this cedar story. The price of cedar shavings is starting to rise, now that the weed-blocking ability of cedar mulch has gone public. But we still pay half as much for cedar as we did for bark dust, with double the good results. I do extend my sympathy to those people who garden far from the cedar mills and forests that supply the beautiful mulches we take for granted here in Washington state. Just as every area has its own native plants, so every area can offer its own native mulches. Cocoa hulls, seaweed, spent hops, peanut shells, and salt hay are other mulching materials available further south, where fir bark and cedar chips are too expensive.

The best mulch for your garden is one that is easily and inexpensively available in your area. If you have a lot of ground to cover, you're going to need a lot of mulch.

Compost — the Mulch from Heaven

Compost is simply rotted plant material. Rich, dark, and good for the soil, a mulch of composted grass clippings and leaves is a beautifully healthy way to smother weeds and conserve on water. Serious gardeners make their own compost from yard clippings fermented in their own backyards.

You can purchase packaged mushroom compost at many garden centers, but be sure to read the label before spreading mushroom compost around all your plants. The composted manure and straw that mushroom farms export may be too high in salts for use around some rhododendrons and azaleas.

In some cities, the park department and sewage treatment plants will get together and build giant compost piles, selling the excess to the public. Composted manure is sold in plastic bags wherever peat moss and potting soil is sold, but buying compost is expensive and inconvenient. You probably have all the ingredients to make compost right in your own backyard.

How to Get Compost the Lazy Way
Composting is a gardening term that every hard-working gardening fanatic is familiar with. There are plenty of shortcuts you can take in making your own compost, even if you don't fall into the category of a hard-working gardener.

You can buy slatted compost bins, rotating compost barrels, and special tools for aerating a steaming compost pile. Most of these products work just fine and help gardeners make more compost with less work. The problem is that the truly lazy gardener will not have the time or muscles to stack, stir, or bother with any of these fine and fancy forms of composting.

Composting on the Spot

There is a method of composting that appeals to the very lazy and the very busy. It's called *spot composting*. Just dig a shallow hole and bury your weeds, leaves, and debris right on the spot. If you already use a mulch on top of your soil, just scrape away the mulch before you dig and then rake the mulch back over your underground compost pile. In a few months, you can plant a shrub or tree in that very same spot and dig into soft, black, composted soil.

I started spot composting when I could no longer find any long blocks of time to garden. Uninterrupted afternoons spent gardening is one luxury that not everyone can afford. When I do get outside, I'm always surrounded by two or three young "helpers." I am forced to start and finish gardening projects in very short blocks of time. Weeding and composting became two jobs I could do at the same time. I pull a weed, and plop it in my bucket; pull another weed or pick off a spent flower, scrape up a few dead leaves, and add all of this to the bucket. I'm usually interrupted before my bucket is full, but that's part of the composting plan. If my bucket of weeds sits ignored for a couple of days, I can be sure all the weeds are dead and dried up before they get buried. When I do return to the garden, I always grab the bucket of dehydrated plant parts, and the first thing I do is dig a little hole to bury the humble remains of my earlier weeding. I don't worry about shaking the soil off my weeds, because that soil will be returned to the garden anyway. I don't need to carry around a heavy shovel, because my weed piles fill only half a bucket once they dry up and shrink. I can use a hand trowel to dig and bury such a small volume of plant material.

My bucket sits right outside the back door, with a hand trowel and gardening gloves stored inside. It's easy to add carrot peelings or other kitchen garbage suitable for composting. Never put meat scraps or leftover food into the composting bucket or you'll be beating the stray animals away from your doorstep. Dried-up potato peelings and uprooted weeds have no odor and attract no animal pests. I'm lucky enough to have a handy spot under the porch steps to hide my bucket, so that my weed collection is always conveniently stored out of sight until I get around to burying it.

I can hear your protests and excuses already. For many gardeners, spot composting just wouldn't work. You say your "soil" is as hard as cement and you need a pickaxe, not a hand trowel, to dig a hole? Add organic matter, and keep that hard soil mulched; it will soften up in a year or two.

Or maybe your style of gardening is to work on the yard one day a month for six hours straight and then ignore the weeds for a month or two. Gardeners who procrastinate until the weeds are thick gather truckloads of weeds in just a few hours, and couldn't possibly bury the piles they collect. Homeowners with established gardens or overgrown yards may have trouble finding an empty spot to dig a hole. The problem with spot composting is that, while it improves the soil, it gives you nothing to use in the garden as a mulch.

So…when there's no unplanted earth left to dig in, when your weed piles are enormous, or when you just don't feel up to digging in your rocky soil, spot composting won't be easy. If it's not easy, it may not seem worth it to the lazy gardener. But composting in some form is important. Composting is cheap, it's efficient, it imitates Mother Nature, and it's good for the environment. I wouldn't be surprised if it also cures cancer and promotes world peace. If spot composting doesn't fit into your lifestyle, there is still another form of composting for lazy gardeners. Keep reading.

Manufacturing Mulch with a "Wait-Awhile" Compost Pile

Long-term composting is another method suitable for laid-back gardeners who want to reap the benefits but not the backaches of a compost pile.

There is nothing to build or buy or study. Just dump all your collected weeds and grass clippings along with some soil into a pile and wait. You can make the piles as big or as small as you wish. Small piles can be hidden behind shrubs or trees. Stick a giant pile out behind a shed or garage. If you layer green material (grass, weeds, or garden clippings) with brown material (soil, manure, sawdust, or peat moss) then all you have to do is water the pile during droughts and otherwise ignore it. In less than a year's time the middle and bottom parts of the pile will have rotted. The dark crumbly material you find in the center of the pile is compost. This rotted plant material is the same compost that some gardeners spend money, time, and muscles making. They may get it quicker, by stirring and aerating and turning their piles, and they may get a lot more of it, with compost activators and rotating drums, but the lazy gardener can have homemade compost without all the hassle. You don't need to understand the chemistry involved in carbon breakdown and heat buildup. Just remember that the green things you add to the pile need to be balanced with brown material to keep the fermenting process active. If you don't have manure or topsoil to throw on the pile, use moist peat moss or brown leaves to counter the green. Good things come to those lazy enough to wait and let nature take its course.

Our long-term compost pile is hidden behind a clump of trees. It grows huge every spring when pruning and garden cleanup swells the pile with weeds and yard clippings, and we make sure it is covered with a layer of soil and brown leaves before summer arrives. Because compost forms quickly in warm weather, the spring pile is ready to use by August. Meanwhile, we have started a new pile for all the grass clippings we collect in the summer. If the grass clippings start to smell or turn slimy, they need to be added in thinner layers so they won't mat down. The brown material we add to the top of every grass layer keeps away the flies and seals in the heat of the rotting process.

In our rainy climate, our pile never needs extra moisture, since it's tucked away in the shade of the trees, but in the fall we cover it with a large piece of plastic. The plastic keeps the warmth in so the pile won't freeze and keeps the constant winter rains out, so that all the nutrients won't get washed away. This four-foot-high by eight-foot-square pile then sits ignored all winter long.

Spring is the time to add mulch to the garden, so in March we unwrap the composted grass clippings and brown leaves and delight in Mother Nature's gift. The top and sides of the pile may still look a little raw, but the inner core of our casually built pile is always rotted and ready to spread as a mulch meal for hungry plants. As the summer progresses, the plants continue to grow and need more pruning, more weeds are collected, and another compost pile builds up so the cycle can begin again.

Rock Mulches: Put the Weeds to Death by Stoning

Gravel comes in many shapes and sizes, but then, so do weeds. A rock mulch can be used to keep down weeds and seal in moisture in the same way that other mulches are used. Rock mulches work best in large areas with few plants, or as transitional borders where pavement or some other hard surface ends and the flower beds begin. A good example is the one-foot-wide border of rock or gravel that lines a driveway or surrounds a deck. This weed-blocking rock border can be used as a base on which to set pots, or as a buffer to keep messy mulches from spilling onto paved areas.

Dry streambeds and gravel pathways are another way to use rocks as a weed block. In areas where no plants will be grown, the lazy gardener can lay black plastic down and put the stone or gravel mulch on top. Poke holes in the plastic for drainage and make sure the rock layer on top is at least two inches thick and completely covers the edges of the plastic undersheeting. Plastic poking up through a gravel path or visible in a dry streambed is considered very bad form, even in a low-maintenance garden. Peek-a-boo plastic in the garden is like a well-dressed woman walking around with her underwear showing.

Volcanic rock, white rock, cinder rock, and crushed marble are all attractive rock forms that can be used for mulching. Remember that crushed rock mulches won't improve the soil like an organic mulch, but they don't have to be replaced as often, either. Lightweight cinder rock or volcanic rock will blow around in a wind-storm, and all rock mulches will collect leaves and debris over time. These are two reasons why a fresh rock layer may need to be added every two or three years to keep the pebbles looking pretty.

Lazy gardeners can benefit from the weed-blocking ability of stepping stones. Use large, flat rocks or manufactured cement squares between your flowers or through your shrubbery. These charming paths not only give you a dry place to put your feet, but they also smother out a good section of weeds. Moss may not grow on a rolling stone, and weeds certainly won't grow under a *stepping* stone.

Living Mulches: Another Name for Groundcover Plants

Groundcover plants take life easy by sprawling around on their bellies. A groundcover plant can be anything that grows with a creeping or spreading form. Lawns are the ultimate in groundcover plants. Many vines and climbing roses can be considered groundcovers, too, if they are left to ramble naturally rather than trained to grow upward with the support of a trellis.

The lazy gardener needs to understand right now that groundcover plants cannot be planted and then ignored. During the first year of life they need to be watered, weeded, and pampered along. In the second year the ground may still be showing between the plants, and more hand-weeding will be necessary. It may take as long as three years for a slow-growing groundcover to completely cover the ground and choke out the weeds.

Once they get going, though, these low-growing plants earn high marks with laid-back gardeners. The easiest-to-grow and best weed-blocking groundcovers are those that grow quick and thick without jumping the barriers of restraint that keep them from becoming nuisance plants. Although no groundcover knows when to stop spreading, some are easier to control than others. Groundcovers with far-reaching vines and invasive root systems should be used only in large, open areas, where they can satisfy their desire to cover the face of the earth.

Use short, ground-hugging plants for smaller areas of the garden or to carpet the ground beneath trees and shrubs. Frugal gardeners should realize that the cost of buying groundcover plants is an investment in lower maintenance that will grow and grow.

Best Groundcovers for the Lazy Gardener

To earn a spot on this list of the easiest-to-grow groundcover plants, each contestant has to have weed-choking abilities, along with a controllable growth habit. Bamboo is one example of a fantastic groundcover that gets carried away with its "conquer-the-world" enthusiasm; it will take over the yard if its roots aren't contained. Because of this rude behavior, bamboo will never be a favorite of the lazy gardener.

These low-maintenance plants also have to demonstrate an easy-going adaptability to soil and weather conditions. Most of these hardy groundcovers will survive winter temperatures of twenty degrees below zero and thrive in almost any type of soil. Some are even recommended for the sandy soil and salt spray of the seashore.

The third trait all these winning weed blockers share is availability. The groundcovers listed are easy to find at your local nursery in the spring, or can be special-ordered for you in mass quantities.

Groundcovers for the Sun and Slope

Cotoneaster: The bearberry cotoneaster is a mild-mannered groundcover for holding the soil on slopes. Cotoneaster doesn't care what kind of soil you plant it in, as long as it drains well. This is one groundcover that will even grow at the seashore. Cotoneaster has shiny, small green leaves, tiny white flowers in the spring, and bright red berries in the fall and winter. If you have rocky soil and want winter color, then cotoneaster is the creeping plant for you. In the early summer, you can snip off cuttings from cotoneaster and root them in a bucket of water. *Weakness:* Cotoneaster is rather slow to get started, and weeds can poke up through a planting for several years. This plant has woody stems like a shrub, so heavy pruning can be heavy work. Give it a large area to cover and you can avoid taking the shears to cotoneaster.

Ivy: Excellent weed-choking abilities put ivy in a league by itself. Ivy is one of the least expensive groundcovers you can buy, since new plants are so easy to start from cuttings off of older plants. Ivy will survive if planted in the deep shade of trees, as well as on sunny banks. Give established ivy beds a good shearing every other spring. By cutting them back to the ground you can revitalize old ivy plantings. *Weakness:* Turn your back for a year or two, and ivy will spill over into the lawn or snake its way up a tree. Ivy needs yearly pruning to keep it contained once it fills up the area. Ivy also likes a moist soil and needs deep watering once a week during hot summers.

Hypericum: This plant is known by two common names: Aaron's beard and St. John's-wort. It's a true sun lover, with sunny yellow flowers and a sunny disposition to match. Not picky about soil or lots of water, this groundcover grows taller (a little more than a foot high) and spreads a bit slower than ivy, but is just as good at blocking out weeds. The flowers are large and continuous throughout most of the summer. A great groundcover for steep slopes or around taller shrubs, it will tolerate light shade. *Weakness:* Hypericum will freeze to death in areas where the temperature falls much below zero, and even in mild winter areas this groundcover may turn black from heavy frost. Once established, hypericum needs to be mowed to the ground early each spring to keep it looking fresh.

Wilton Carpet Juniper: A ground-hugging juniper that has beautiful blue needles. Don't overfertilize or water too much, or the foliage will turn green. Good drought resistance, and it tolerates sandy soil, extremely cold winters (to forty degrees below zero), hot sun, and light shade. *Weakness:* Junipers in general are often overused in the landscape, and so they have a reputation as being rather boring plants. Wilton is a juniper that is very hard to kill, and this trait is more important than lush good looks to many gardeners. Another problem with using juniper as a groundcover shrub is that it grows more slowly than the more viny plants and needs a thick mulch around it to keep down the weeds.

Creeping Thyme: A great-smelling, sun-loving groundcover that hugs the ground just like a gray wool carpet. A little hand-weeding may be needed each spring, but most weeds will be smothered by the passing creep of thyme. Thyme is the perfect plant to use between stepping stones or to spill over large rocks. New plantings are simple to make by dividing old clumps with a garden trowel. *Weakness:* Thyme is a perennial herb, not a sprawling shrub, and does not have the woody stems and root system that will control erosion on a slope. Best for smaller areas because of the yearly hand-weeding it requires.

Best Places to Plant Groundcovers

Any place that is hard to mow, in deep shade, or seldom seen should sport some groundcover other than a lawn. Here are some classic spots for classic groundcovers:

- Slopes and steep inclines
- Under trees
- Narrow spaces up next to the house
- Dry, wet, or difficult areas where nothing else wants to grow

Groundcovers for the Shade:

Vinca minor: This vinelike evergreen has spring flowers of lovely periwinkle blue, and so it is often called by its common name, periwinkle. Add peat moss to the soil before you plant vinca, give it plenty of water during droughts, and it will grow to delight you. Perfect for planting under trees and shrubs, and, since it's shallow-rooted, you can plant bulbs amongst the periwinkle and then tuck the spent foliage neatly under the vinca covering after the flowers bloom. Take cuttings from the plants in the spring to spread vinca all over your yard. *Weakness:* Vinca has a nasty habit of turning yellow if it doesn't get what it wants in the way of nutrients. You may need to fertilize with a rhododendron and azalea food if it starts to act up.

Ajuga: Just listen to the common name of this plant, "carpet bugle," and then picture a carpet of golden-green plants heralded with trumpets of deep blue flowers in the spring. Ajuga will bloom in the deepest of shade and it spreads fast. If you improve the soil with peat moss or other organic matter before you plant, then keep the soil moist all summer, you will have a solid mass planting by fall — even if you space new plants a foot apart. Few weeds can penetrate a thick patch of ajuga, and it dies back naturally in the winter, so it never needs a spring mowing to keep it fresh. Increase your ajuga plants by chopping off the new young plants that form at the ends of runners. *Weakness:* Ajuga has runners that may jump the borders of restraint and try to infest your lawn and flower beds. Hardy to twenty degrees below zero, but needs lots of water and shade in dry climates.

Pachysandra: This evergreen groundcover has handsome, shiny green leaves and tiny white flowers in the spring. It is tough enough to survive in the deep shade of trees, but needs extra water and fertilizing to get it started in such hostile locations. Pachysandra starts out slowly, but once established will block out weeds and shade its own roots, so you won't need to water as often. Space the plants six inches apart and propagate by dividing up the roots in early spring or taking stem cuttings. Pachysandra can be used to control erosion on shady hillsides. If you want a neat and tidy groundcover as uniform as an emerald green lawn, then pachysandra will grow to please you. *Weakness:* Pachysandra needs a slightly acid soil and turns yellow if you don't meet that demand. Add plenty of peat moss to the soil before planting.

Getting in on the Ground Floor: Purchase and Installation

Buying groundcover plants should be done in the spring. Pay more for the biggest plants you can find, because then you'll be able to divide a single plant into two or more smaller plants and cover more ground.

Because groundcover plants grow so quickly, they are also very easy for the laziest gardener to propagate. All of the plants recommended above can be started from cuttings. Taking cuttings from a groundcover plant is very simple. Just cut off a hunk of tip growth and, if there are any roots attached, you can plant the severed section right where you want it to grow. Keep the soil moist until new roots form.

Groundcovers with thick and woody stems can be rooted easily in water. I planted a steep bank with cotoneaster one spring, and the following year took cuttings from the year-old plants. I removed the lower leaves from the bottom half of the one-foot whips I had cut, then stuck that leafless end in a bucket of water. In a few weeks I could see roots forming, so I waited another month and then planted the cuttings into the hillside between the mother plants. The new cotoneaster plants took hold quickly and had filled in the bare spots by the following year.

What to Do Before You Plant

The groundcover plants recommended may tolerate very poor soil, but you'll be paid back quickly for any soil preparation you provide. If your soil has too much clay and packs down as hard as cement, add peat moss. If your soil is sandy or gravelly and won't hold any moisture, add peat moss. If you really want to pamper the new plants, add compost or steer manure. Improving the soil will definitely be appreciated, but perhaps the kindest move of all would be to get rid of the weeds.

New plants, even vigorous groundcover plants have a tough time competing with established grasses and weeds. Use black plastic or a very thick mulch if you have plenty of time to kill off the existing plant growth in the area you have chosen for groundcover plants. Check out Chapter Ten for details on smothering weeds. Hand-weeding is the easiest way to handle small areas in need of clearing.

Once the ground is cleared and the soil amended, just dig a shallow hole and stuff in the roots of your groundcover plant. Now anchor that plant securely in the ground, especially if you're planting on a slope.

Our first home had a backyard too steep for even four-footed creatures to navigate. We know this because we used to gaze out the window and watch the wildlife slide down the cliff. We terraced the slope into three level areas, using lots of railroad ties to form retaining walls. This left lots of steeply sloping ground behind those walls that needed covering. It was while planting groundcovers on that very steep slope that I learned (the hard way) about anchoring plants. My carefully planted groundcovers would wash down the hill with the first rainstorm, until I learned to drop anchor around every plant. Simply digging a shelf instead of a hole in the side of the hill helped a lot. A shelf is just a mini terrace carved out of the hillside. Using a hand trowel, I scooped soil from above the planting spot and piled it in front of the hole, which angled downward and inward into the slope. (See illustration.) This gave the new roots a level spot on which to start growing and captured the runoff water from the rains, routing it into the planting hole instead of straight down our mountainside.

In case you were wondering, the groundcovers finally took hold and took off, stabilizing the hillside and halting any further erosion. We planted ivy, cotoneas-

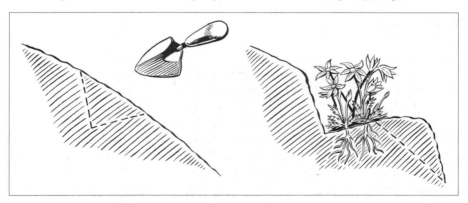

Anchoring a plant on a hillside or steep slope. Dig a hole angled downward and inward into the slope (left). Then pile the soil you've removed in front of the hole to create a mini terrace (right).

ter, and juniper, to see what kind of groundcover would do best in our rocky soil and partial shade. All three groundcovers thrived, and in three years the sloping banks were beautifully covered and maintenance-free. I pulled a few lonely weeds from the slope each spring, but the vigorous groundcovers and a bark mulch choked out the rest.

Spacing Groundcover Plants

The closer you plant, the sooner the ground will be covered, but the more plants you will need. A place to start is one plant per square foot of ground. Plants with long, spreading arms like ivy and cotoneaster can go two feet apart, while tiny ground-hugging covers like creeping thyme or Irish moss should be set six inches apart. Don't forget that you can propagate off of your original plants in a year or so to fill in the bare spots.

Controlling Groundcover Plants

Clipping back the strays is the way most gardeners take care of groundcovers that go wandering, but in a few years you'll need to take a firmer hand with the discipline. Here are some options:

■ Set up a barrier. Bricks, rocks, landscaping timbers — any type of border that would edge a lawn can be used to keep your groundcover in line.

■ Behead the rebels. Run your mowing machine or weed wacker around the edge of the planting a couple times of year. This will work best on soft new growth.

■ Grow the groundcover planting in a raised bed, so that trailing extensions will be easy to snip off as they hang over the raised bed's border.

■ Keep sharing. Trim off the excess to give away or add to other parts of the garden.

A Garden of Groundcovers

Since groundcovers are such time-savers for the lazy gardener, it's only right to design a garden around them. Visit a few groundcovers at your local nursery before you adopt those special ones that you'll want to plan a landscape around. A yard full of groundcovers will need trees and shrubs for height and balance, but you can still enjoy a variety of colors, textures, and flowers when the ground is covered with plants as relaxed and laid-back about gardening as you are.

One of my favorite landscaping ideas for a groundcover is to use creeping woolly thyme instead of water to make a "stream" through the landscape. Use large, flat stones along the edges of the stream for a realistic look and to keep the thyme from overflowing the banks. Go ahead and scrape off the topsoil to give your stream a depression to flow in; creeping thyme prefers poor soil to rich soil. Add a small bridge or stepping stones across the wavy blue-green sea of thyme. You'll have the peaceful tranquility of a babble-free brook.

Our brook of woolly thyme is not the only place we use this living carpet. The rose garden has a walk of stepping stones running through it, and woolly thyme is the perfect groundcover to use around stepping stones. We let the thyme carpet the ground around the roses, and it doesn't seem to bother them a bit. The shallow roots of this groundcover don't interfere with the deep-rooted roses. The woolly carpet now replaces bark chips as a mulch for our roses. We do have to rip this groundcover away from the drip line to fertilize every spring, but thyme is easy to pull away from the soil.

There is a pink-flowering relative called mother-of-thyme that we recently introduced around more roses. Since mother-of-thyme is a spring bloomer, it gives needed color to the rose garden in May.

Most-Asked Mulching and Groundcover Questions

Q. *The ivy that is planted as a groundcover in our landscape looks old and ugly. It has very thick, woody stems, and I know that rodents spend the winter in this mess. What can be done about it?*
A. What your ivy bed needs to wake it up is a good hatchet job. A severe pruning will encourage fresh new vines get rid of those woody stems that attract the vermin. If you don't own a power hedge-clipper, rent one. Cut the vines back clear to the ground. Spread a compost or bark mulch over the area and wait for the flush of tidy new growth. This job is best done in the spring, when all groundcovers could do with a little haircut.

Q. *We had hypericum planted on a sunny slope, and it was doing fine until last winter, when it suffered from a big freeze. There is new growth starting to sprout, but the whole bank looks very sad. How can we speed up the recovery?*
A. Try a lawn mower or string trimmer to cut back all the frozen tops of your hypericum. Fertilize, water, and mulch the bank, and you'll have the ground covered with a bed of fresh growth in a couple of months.

Q. *I am having trouble with my compost pile. I may not be adding enough soil or manure, because things don't decay. The same leaves and branches I put in the pile last fall were waiting for me in the spring. I would like to add that, since I live in the city, manure and extra soil are something we have to pay for.*
A. If your compost is the pits, consider burying it in one. A large hole filled with

composting materials solves several problems. First, by digging a hole, you acquire a pile of soil conveniently located next to the composting pit. Second, the hole in the ground will keep your compost warmer in the winter and cooler in the summer. When your compost pile freezes, it stops working. Third, your compost will be hidden from view and less attractive to pests. Once you have a storehouse of soil, be sure to cover any green material like grass clippings or weeds with a soil layer. Spread the green stuff (nitrogenous material) very thinly, about one inch thick, and the brown stuff (carbon material) at least three inches deep or more. Besides soil you should add leaves, fine bark, or sawdust to bulk up your brown material. Use your lawn mover to chop up the leaves for your pile into small pieces. The smaller the chunks that go into the pile, the quicker it turns into compost.

Q. *I can get sawdust really cheap, but hate to use it as mulch because it turns the plants yellow. How can I use sawdust in a compost pile?*
A. Pile your sawdust next to the compost pile and layer it with grass clippings and other green material. In a few months you should have a nice dark mulch for your garden that won't rob your plants of nitrogen and turn them yellow the way plain sawdust does.

CHAPTER TEN

Plant Problems: The Lazy Way to Deal with Bugs, Weeds, and Disease

The lazy gardener does not have the time, energy, or patience to play nursemaid to a crop of sickly plants. If you want to amass a wealth of healthy plants, then you have to invest in preventive gardening practices. Spend more time keeping your plants healthy, instead of wasting your time treating plants that get sick.

There are times when nothing you can do will prevent bug infestations or devastation from disease. Certain plants are more susceptible to pests, while others suffer greatly due to unusual weather conditions. The lazy gardener must come to terms with the fact that sometimes the most practical approach to treating severely damaged plants is to simply throw them away.

Knowing when to give up and throw in the trowel (and throw out the plant) and when to try and save a sick plant can be difficult . You'll have to consider how much time and energy you are willing to invest, how much you really like the plant, and whether or not the plant's problem is a freak occurrence or one that will return to haunt you year after year.

This chapter is written as a guide to the conscience of a lazy gardener. Plants are not people, after all, and there is a limit to how much should be done to save a plant's life. If you think throwing out a sick plant is a waste of money, wait until you see how much the medicine and equipment for fixing it runs you. Lazy gardeners can call it a Murder of Mercy — the ultimate solution to any problem afflicting your plants.

Ways to Prevent Problems

■ Keep your garden clean. Tall weeds and overripe flowers attract all sorts of problems. Nip off dead flowers, sweep up your pruning crumbs, and pull out the weeds.

■ Water works wonders. A well-watered plant has a strong defense system that wards off many pests. Whenever you let a tree, shrub, or tiny plant feel the stress of thirst, the time becomes ripe for a hostile takeover. Spider mites, aphids, and a host of diseases are all attracted to weak and wilting plant life. Too much water is also an invitation to disaster. Soggy soil encourages disease and fungal infections. Pay attention to the watering needs of your plants.

■ Overfertilizing causes an overabundance of soft green growth. Succulent green growth is more susceptible to frost, insect, and disease damage. Keep your plants well fed, but not overfed. Use a little less chemical fertilizer than the label recommends. Improve your soil with organic matter and you won't have to worry about fertilizing so much with chemicals.

■ Give your plants room to breathe. Good air circulation is especially important in shady, moist sections of your yard. The steaming jungle is also a teeming bundle of bugs. Avoid the overcrowded jungle look. Thin out and throw out overgrown plant life. Opening up the garden also allows the antiseptic rays of the sun to pass through.

■ You can probably avoid ninety percent of your plant problems if you just put the right plant in the right place. Plants that are grown in the soil, weather, and light conditions that they love are plants without problems. Yes, I know, that's an easy piece of advice to give, but very hard to live by. Try to use your head and save your back. Read, research, and remember to ask questions about every plant you consider adding to your garden.

The laziest way to accomplish this task is to describe your planting spot to the experienced personnel at your local nursery or garden center. Instead of buying a plant and then figuring out where to locate it, choose a location and let them figure out what kind of plant would most like to grow there.

Murders of Mercy: How to Decide When It's Time for the Axe

Any time a plant in your garden is struggling with a problem, you should investigate immediately and take prompt action to keep little irritations from turning into big problems. Hard-working, experienced gardeners use this technique of "immediate intervention" quite often and rarely lose a plant.

Now, let's be realistic and admit what often happens in the yard of a lazy gardener. Even if the problem gets noticed right away, it is just too inconvenient to treat the problem immediately. If anything, the sick plant might get a bit of first aid in the form of a quick and convenient treatment of some kind. Lazy gardeners are not about to buy special sprays and administer them weekly or fumigate the soil. They're much more likely to hope for the best and do nothing at all.

Sometimes this hands-off, laid-back approach works out fine. Often the plant only goes from sick to dead. The sick plant may punish you further by taking its time to slowly suffer an ugly and painful death. You can sit by and watch the process and feel terribly guilty about not taking heroic measures to save the plant, or you can do the merciful thing and swiftly put the poor plant out of its misery by pulling it out of your garden.

Mercy killing should not be a shocking idea to lazy gardeners. It also should not be a murder committed lightly. You don't want to get carried away and uproot every yellowing shrub or bloomless flowering plant. Murders of mercy should be committed only on plants that are seriously ill. Dig up the rose that has turned leafless because of black spot, or the rhododendron in a black and permanent wilt from root decay. Give up on the hanging fuchsia that has yellowing leaves and a cloud of whiteflies swarming around it. Throw out the snapdragons and hollyhocks riddled with rust and the juniper plants turning orange from spider mites. Yes, it may be possible to save these plants if you spray them several times at certain intervals and invest in chemicals and equipment, but just because it's possible to save a plant doesn't mean it's always worth it.

One of the golden rules of lazy gardening is to go with the flow and plant only what loves to grow in your yard. A seriously sick plant is not showing great adaptability to your yard and lifestyle. Any plant that grows too demanding for a lazy gardener doesn't deserve to live. There is no room for guilt in the garden. Plants are grown for your enjoyment, and if you don't enjoy picking bugs or spraying fungicides, then the infested plant is not performing up to expectations and deserves to lose the privilege of growing in your yard.

Sound too harsh and unforgiving? Okay then, give the sick plant one more chance to redeem itself with a single, simple attempt at treatment. If the patient doesn't take a turn for the better, off with its head.

Check these signs of distress and dump the plant that's guilty of three out of these four deadly sins:

1. Plant (or tree or shrub) looks awful, even when viewed from a distance.

2. Plant shows no signs of new growth.

3. More than half the plant is afflicted and showing signs of decline.

4. You've been fighting the problem for a month or more and it just keeps getting worse.

Here are four facts that help make mercy killings easier to perform. Repeat these lines over and over while you march on out and end the silent suffering of all the sick plants in your garden:

1. A sick plant could easily spread its infection to other healthy plants in the garden. Better to lose one plant in the beginning than a dozen later on.

2. Once a wimp, almost always a wimp. Even if you succeed in keeping the mildew or mites under control this summer, you'll still be stuck with a susceptible plant next year, and the year after that. You could win the battle but get stuck with a lifetime of war.

3. Nursing along a sickly plant eats up time, energy, and money. A lazy gardener may end up neglecting the weeding, watering, and feeding in the rest of the yard if too much energy gets spent on one demanding specimen. Time and energy spent in the garden is precious. Spend it where it will do the most good for the greatest number of plants. You won't have time to practice prevention if you're busy taking heroic measures to save plants whose time to go has come.

4. Sick plants are unsightly. Your garden should be a beautiful and peaceful place. One dying tree can blight an entire landscape, one chewed-up petunia can spoil a whole flower bed. Better dead and gone than a suffering scene spoiler.

Don't Forget to Try a Transplant!

Sometimes a change in the scenery brings about a positive change in attitude. Any plant giving you trouble or just not performing as it should can be moved to a new location for a fresh start. If it's in the shade, move it where it will get more sun. If it's growing in a low, wet spot, try it where it will be high and dry. Dig a lot of peat moss or compost into the new planting hole. Christen it with plenty of water and warn it to shape up, or else its next move will be to the garbage can.

Early Warnings — Nip the Problems in the Bud

If you can force yourself to move quickly at the first sign of trouble, you won't be euthanizing as many plants. Sometimes all it takes is to pluck off a few diseased leaves or hand-pick a few bugs to end the start of a fatal attraction. Pay attention and really look at your plants every chance you get. You'll not only notice their problems a lot sooner, you'll also learn to appreciate all the rich details of their beauty.

The section below includes eight of the most common "first alert" warning signs for a plant in trouble. After the symptom is a list of possible causes and some steps you can take to administer first aid. These first-aid suggestions are purposely simplified. This is because the lazy gardener may never get around to an elaborate identification and treatment of the problem, but may take the time to do something as simple as watering or washing the plant.

Let me warn you that these easy and simplified first-aid solutions will not ensure a miracle cure, and there's a good chance that they won't help at all. These first-aid measures can prolong a plant's life, however, and may control the problem until either: 1) you can get some professional advice; 2) the plant rallies and improves; or 3) you decide to permanently end the suffering by ending the life of the plant.

Warning Signs to Watch for, Possible Causes, and First-Aid Suggestions

Dropping leaves. Check for lack of water, mites, wet and rotten roots. *Treatment:* Wash the plant; dig into the soil to check for dryness or excessive wetness.

Pale coloring or change in leaf color. Could be sunburn or not enough light. Could also be over- or underfertilization. Mites may be feeding on the back of the foliage. *Treatment:* Check for mites, wash with mild soap; consider fertilizing with a fast-acting liquid food. Add or take away shade.

Bite marks or ragged holes in foliage. Look for chewing insects like caterpillars or slugs. *Treatment:* Pluck them off.

Shriveled new growth. Could be disease or lack of water, cold temperatures, or root problems. *Treatment:* Clip off unsightly sections; check for dry soil.

Sticky or sooty black leaves. Suspect aphids. The sticky stuff is the honeydew they excrete. The black film is just mold growing on the sticky dew. Be suspicious of overhead branches that may be hosting the drippy aphids. *Treatment:* Hose down trees or wash plants with soapy water.

Black or scorched look to the foliage. Usually some kind of disease. *Treatment:* Clip off damaged sections.

Spots, mold, or blotches on the leaves. All kinds of disease and some types of insects can cause funny leaf spots. *Treatment:* Remove the worst-looking leaves. Clean up debris around the plant. Try to increase air circulation.

Plant doesn't grow, looks listless. Lack of water, lack of nutrients, compacted soil. *Treatment:* Check for dry soil; try a liquid plant food; loosen the soil with shallow cultivation.

When First Aid Fails — More Help for Valuable Plants

Plant problems can be complex. Your sick plant could be suffering from a multitude of problems or be slowly dying from an ailment that remains a total mystery to even the experienced gardener. The lazy gardener needs to know how to get help fast and easily. Luckily there are plenty of plant professionals in most communities who make a practice out of practicing medicine on practically dead plants. There's the garden manager at your local garden center, the owner of the neighborhood nursery, the county extension agent, the neighborhood gardening expert, and even the person who writes the gardening column for your local newspaper. These people are happy to help, don't charge you for their advice, and are only a phone call away. What more could the lazy gardener want? Yes, I know, you want *accuracy*, and it is very possible that three different experts will give you three different causes for your plant's problem. Remember that, just like a medical doctor, plant doctors can only "practice" medicine. Nobody yet as "perfected" the art of diagnosis and treatment.

As a garden columnist, I am bombarded with plant-care questions. To tell you the truth, I am still delighted every time a reader writes to me about a plant problem and something I suggest actually helps the poor plant. Diagnosing health problems through the mail is like playing baseball in the dark. There's a fair chance you might score big, but you also strike out a lot.

Nothing beats a house call (yard call?) for accurate diagnosis, but the next best thing is to take the patient (or at least bring a piece of the patient) into the doctor's office. Bring a branch or leaf and a soil sample from around the plant when you go for help. The more information you bring the experts, the more accurate their prescription will be.

The Golden Rule for Bug Control

The battle of the bug has been waged for centuries. We'll probably go on fighting with the bugs over our plants for as long as we both inhabit the earth. The hardest part of bug control is punishing the bad bugs without harming the good insects. Step on a big black beetle and, not only will you hear a sickening crunch, but your plants will be devoured by slugs and snails as further punishment. You see, that shiny black beetle was probably out searching for its favorite dinner — slug and snail eggs.

Gardeners who are quick to pound every insect they see hanging around the garden need to repeat this little line before beheading another beetle: *If it moves slowly, kill it. If it moves quickly, leave it alone.*

The slow-moving bugs are usually plant eaters, while the fast movers more often than not are the meat-eating hunters, searching for the sluggish vegetarian bugs that hide around your plants. There are lots of exceptions to this rule, so if you meet a quick-steeping weevil, and you know it's been chewing on your shrubs, stomp on it quick before it gets away.

Weapons to Do Battle with the Bug

Aphid pinch: Just use your two pinching fingers and squish the aphid colonies you see on the tip growth of your plants. Like any experienced murderer, I always wear gloves when committing this act. I don't care about leaving my fingerprints at the scene of the crime—it's just that squashed aphids are so sticky.

Water torture: When the aphid colonies are numerous, or the infested plant is a large tree or shrub, a forceful stream of water can wash away a lot of bugs in a little time. If you hit the jackpot and notice swarms of bugs wriggling on the ground after a jet-stream bath, throw buckets of soapy water on top of the survivors. Most insects have a waxy coating on their bodies that is worn away by soapsuds. Soaping up a bug is a lot like skinning it alive. That will teach those critters to mess with your favorite plants.

Caterpillar catchers: Eyebrow tweezers or your own nimble fingers make good worm pluckers for those cases when you confront something chewing on the foliage of your plants. Early morning is the best time to catch these feasting insects in the act. When caterpillars congregate on the tips of branches, prune off the most infected sections. Submerge the branch in water or burn the amputated limbs.

Sticky tape: Nothing to mix or spray—just peel off a protective layer and hang these bright yellow strips on your plants that are bothered by flying insects like whitefly. The yellow color draws the tiny bugs closer until they become hopelessly mired in the tacky glue. The same principle as old-fashioned flypaper, and just as easy for the lazy gardener to use. Sticky yellow tape designed for bug control is sold at large garden centers.

Slug traps: When you garden in a cool, shady spot, slugs and snails will devour your plants almost overnight. Slug bait comes in several forms, from liquid to granular, and all are in an easy, ready-to-use form. These types of bait work well, but if you're too cheap, lazy, or organic to buy slug bait from a store, you can make your own.

Just set a shallow saucer of beer in the garden and wait for the drunkards to drown in their intoxicated state. You could also leave a wet piece of cardboard in the area for all the slugs to sleep under. Lure them to the hiding place with a piece of beer-soaked bread. In the morning you can collect the slimy critters and dispose of them neatly by dropping the cardboard into the garbage.

Ready-to-use trigger spray pesticides: There are complete lines of pesticides that are ready to use and require no mixing, measuring, or special equipment. These are pesticides made for the lazy gardener. You don't even have to worry about ruining the environment, because organic bug-killing sprays and fungicides also come in ready-to-use form.

I'll admit you do pay more for the convenience of the one-step spray, but if you examine your conscience, you may admit that you will never get around to using something that needs to be measured and mixed. Are those bargain products that come in bulk really a bargain if you don't use them? Much easier (and much more likely to get done) is to aim a spray bottle armed with a pre-mixed pesticide at the enemy and just pull the trigger. When you're short on time and energy, it pays to pay for convenience.

Defense from Disease

The gamut of plant disease is almost as horrendous and horrifying as human pathology. The lazy gardener should consult reference books or gardening experts for treatment of disease on very valuable plants. The bad news is that many plant infections cannot be cured with a single shot of plant medicine fired from a trigger-spray bottle. Many plant diseases are caused by fungal infections. A fungicide kills fungus disease spores that cause black spot, powdery mildew, and a host of other problems. A fungicide will not control bacterial and viral disease, however. Even conquering a fungal disease often takes many treatments.

The good news is that most diseases are weather-related. Cool, moist weather and hot, humid weather increase the chances of an epidemic, so a change in the weather can slow the spread of the disease. Sometimes this weather change helps a relatively healthy plant to combat the infection on its own. In other words, if you do nothing at all, minor disease infections may disappear because of the vigor of your plant.

Here's what you can do to help your plants fight disease on their own:

■ At the first sign of trouble, remove any infected leaves or cut off any damaged branches several inches from the start of the infection.

■ Clean up fallen debris, especially leaves from around the sick plant.

■ Prune nearby plants if practical to give the patient maximum air circulation and sunlight. Do not use the same pruning equipment you used on the sick plant until it has been disinfected in a strong bleach solution.

■ Do not fertilize an obviously diseased or distressed plant. It has enough to worry about without digesting a heavy dose of plant food.

■ Do not overwater a sick plant, but don't let the soil get dry, either. Sick plants use less water than healthy growing plants, so you may not need to water as often as before.

■ Seriously consider a mercy killing of any plant with a disease that begins to spread throughout the garden. At the very least move it to an isolated area — it may just like the new location enough to fend off the disease on its own.

■ Try pruning back your sickly plants almost to the ground. Leaving a few leafless stumps may be the only way an infected plant can escape its tormentors and turn over a healthy new leaf.

■ Wait for winter to move in, and perhaps the enemy will freeze to death. The infected plant may get a fresh start next spring. Just make sure you clean up all the debris in the fall.

Weed Wars:
Lazy Ways to Fight This Never-Ending Battle

Even if you take good care of your garden, improve the soil, and irrigate and fertilize, you'll still get weeds. The truth is that a weed is simply a plant you don't want growing in your yard. Some gardeners plant wildflower seeds, while others spend time rooting out the wildflowers that volunteer. Morning glory is welcomed in some gardens as a lovely blooming vine, and cursed in others as an invasive weed.

I always chuckle when I remember the day I appeared at a local nursery to answer spring gardening questions. One woman brought in a hunk of emerald green moss and asked how she could kill it. The moss was growing all over her flower beds and spreading into her lawn. I assured her the moss was not harming the plants and that it should be easy to scrape off and cart away to the compost pile.

The very next woman in line with a gardening question had a stream running through her backyard. She wanted to know where she could find some moss to plant amongst the rocks down by the stream. I leaped toward the exit to catch the first lady with the moss-covered yard, who was just leaving. The two women were delighted to help each other out. The moss-loving lady followed the moss-hating woman home and helped herself to all the moss she could muster into her car. One garden's weeds is another garden's wonder.

If you don't know of any gardeners who are dying to dig up your weeds and take them away, you'll just have to take care of the problem yourself. Here are the best ways for the lazy gardener to enjoy a reasonably weed-free garden.

■ Use a mulch to smother the problem. The thicker, the better. Check Chapter Nine for the lowdown on low-maintenance mulches.

■ Improve and water the soil only where you need to. If you have lousy, barren soil, keep it that way and you'll have fewer weeds to fight. Instead of hauling in topsoil and covering your planting beds with two or three inches of weed-producing soil, just dig big holes whenever you plant something and replace the poor soil with good soil. You'll only have pockets of good soil to weed instead of a yardful.

The same idea works with irrigation. Use a drip system to water just the root zones of your desirable plants. The rest of the soil will remain too dry for many weed seeds to sprout.

■ Make new friends. Learn to like a few weeds. Turn your large lawn into a blooming meadow and call anything that blooms uninvited a wildflower. If you really want to impress the neighbors, call your weed-filled yard a protected preserve for rare wildflowers and native plants.

■ Use newspaper and smother weeds with words. Lay down newspapers in five-to ten-page sections. Sprinkle the paper with water to keep it from blowing around on windy days. Now cover the newspaper weed block with a mulch or fresh layer of topsoil. Newspaper works great for smothering those thousands of annual weeds that are too numerous to pull by hand, too close to your other plants to spray with a weed killer, and too full of seedpods to just hoe into the soil. Newspaper is plentiful, biodegradable, and affordable.

Here's an easy way to make a new planting bed in a sea of lawn. Cover the grass with a newspaper layer and then just dump topsoil in a mound on top. Use stones or landscaping timbers to outline the bed and contain the raised bed of soil. Now you can add shallow-rooted shrubs and flowers instantly. By the time the plant roots grow down deep, the newspaper will have decomposed and the sod below will have been composted. Sodbusting should be a pain of the past as long as there are newspapers around.

■ Use cardboard. Cardboard boxes knock down in a jiffy, and a sheet of thick cardboard, weighted down so that it lies close to the earth, can smother to death the hardiest weeds. Moving into a new house? Put those packing boxes to work once they're emptied. Use cardboard instead of chemicals to clear a path, smother sections of weed for a new lawn, or eliminate groundcovers gone wild. Thick cardboard can be laid out, sprinkled with water, and then immediately covered with an attractive mulch for instant good looks in overgrown weed patches.

■ Use a woven weed-block material beneath your mulch. The woven weed blocks allow air and water to pass through, but no weeds can sneak up. The high price tag on some of these landscaping fabrics reflects the fact that these materials last many years as silent sentinels, keeping a lid on the weed explosion. Some are made of woven plastic, others feel more like felt. All are a good investment.

■ Weeds in cracks of the sidewalk or patio? Pour boiling salt water into the cracks to not only kill the weeds, but keep them from coming back.

■ Hoe up weeds early in the morning when hot weather is in the forecast. Leave the weeds lying on top of the soil with their roots exposed. By evening, the sun will have dried the life right out of those weeds, and they'll be easy to rake into a pile for composting or burying in the garden beds.

Easier yet, hoe out your weeds a few days before you spread a new layer of mulch. Let the weeds lie where they are while the sun thoroughly dries their roots and tops. Now just spread the new mulch on top of the withered weeds and they'll decompose and return something to the garden they were caught robbing.

■ Use a sharp pointed hoe on those tiny little weeds that sprout among your seedlings. The thin blade of the pointed hoe can reach under the soil to slice the weedlings from their roots. Do this before you thin your seedlings. Your little hoeing mistakes that damage the planted seedlings instead of the weeds won't be so upsetting, since the new plants need to be thinned anyway. Anytime a lazy gardener can avoid hand-pulling weeds, it's worth a few seedling casualties.

■ Ready, aim, and fire with a hand-held weed spray. You can shoot to kill in your own backyard. Thanks to the organic movement there are now liquid weed killers that are safe for the environment. The Safer company makes an organic weed spray that shows results in just a few hours! Sprays that kill plant life are called herbicides. (I always picture a dead man named Herb lying in the aisle next to the plant-killing chemicals.) Some of these products can knock down blackberries and other tough-to-handle weeds. They can also kill your desirable plants. Read the next chapter on gardening horror stories before you make the decision to use chemical weed killers.

There's an armory of weed-fighting artillery out there on your garden center's shelves. You should feel a little guilty if you have to resort to chemical warfare. Rely on mulch and manual labor whenever possible and avoid the hassle, headaches, and heartaches of expensive weed-killing chemicals.

Most-Asked Disease, Insect, and Weed Questions

Q. *I've tried mulching with bark dust, and the weeds still come up in my garden. I have a big yard and I hate to weed. Any suggestions?*
A. Pile on a thicker mulch. You can mulch six to eight inches deep around trees and most shrubs, but don't mulch that deep right up next to the trunk of shallow-rooted shrubs like rhododendrons, azaleas, and camellias. If you don't have access to a lot of mulch, lay down newspapers and spread a two-inch layer of mulch on top. Add gravel pathways, groundcovers, stepping stones, and other hard surfaces to your landscape, so the weeds won't have as many places to poke up.

Q. *What can I do about really tough weeds like Canada thistle and horsetail? When I try to pull them out, they just come galloping back thicker then ever! They even break through my thick mulch and are invading all my garden beds. Help!*
A. Help is on the way! Canada thistle and horsetail are perennial weeds, which means they return every year, so do not attempt to pull them out by their roots. If you leave even a piece of root, they will multiply. Do not hoe or cultivate either — you are just spreading more root pieces around. What you *can* do is cut the weeds off a few inches below the surface of the soil. Keep cutting the tops off these weeds as they resprout so that the roots have no foliage in the sunlight to manufacture food. If you persistently whack at these weeds when they sprout, the roots will starve after one season.

There are some weed-killing sprays that are safe for the environment and effective against very stubborn weeds. Sharpshooter is the trade name of a soap-based spray made by the Safer company, mentioned earlier, and Roundup and Kleenup are trade names of weed killers made with glyphosate salts that are harmless to people. These weed killers murder all plant life, not just weeds, and you may need to use a paintbrush to spread these liquid herbicides on weeds that are sandwiched in between your desirable plants. Persistence will pay off, so good luck!

Q. *I have some rose plants that have "striped" yellow and green leaves. Light yellow splotches also appear on the foliage, and I was told they have a viral infection. What can I do for viral disease?*
A. Brace yourself for some tragic news. There is no cure for viral disease in plants. Uproot your roses and throw them away. Take a moment to mourn your loss and then replace the holes in your garden with hardier, more disease-resistant roses. Only buy roses from a reputable grower, to avoid introducing such heartbreaking problems to your garden.

Q. *The bugs are overtaking our garden. I tried using some soapy water on the plants, but it doesn't seem to work on the aphids, whiteflies, and other insects eating my plants. What can be done about a plague of insects?*
A. You need to pull out the big guns for bad insect invasions. Soapy water that you mix up yourself with a few drops of mild dishwashing soap is not as effective as the insecticidal soaps that you can purchase ready to use. Insecticidal soaps work best early in the season and need to be applied every couple of days for several weeks to control big outbreaks. These soaps must contact the skin of the insect, so make certain you spray the undersides of the leaves and the ground where the bugs may fall.

There are also stronger poisons like pyrethrum and rotenone that are made from natural products, but they wipe out all the insects in your garden, even the good guys. Use these insecticides if necessary, but then figure out a way to prevent such problems in the future. Install a watering system, improve your soil, do a better job of fertilizing, and plant more resistant flowers. Prevention is the lazy way to do battle with the bugs.

CHAPTER ELEVEN

Gardening Horror Stories

Get ready to be scared right out of your gardening gloves. This chapter is written so that common gardening mistakes will be easier to remember and less often repeated. These gardening horror stories are collected from my landscaping clients, my readers, my friends, and my own foolish mistakes. Although the stories you are about to read are true, the names have been changed to protect the embarrassed. Please note that many of these horrible horticultural blunders are my very own. I figure that fessing up to my own planting errors might ease the worry lines on the brows of beginning gardeners out there. Budding gardeners need to get their hands dirty and just dig in. Never let a few mistakes prune back a growing enthusiasm. Everybody goofs in the garden — some people just won't admit it.

Remember that gardening is an art, not an exact science. Gardeners must have the confidence to try new plants and new designs. Accept the fact that plants will die, grow too large, or just look ugly. Mourn a little, then go on with your gardening. Pull up your mistakes and try again. A garden is not static and should be constantly changing.

One more reading tip. There's a short garden lesson or moral at the end of each sad story. Be sure to read over the lesson twice, so you can avoid repeating the same mistake.

The Case of the Midnight Murders

I am the one guilty of plant murder in this story. It all started in my very first garden when I was about twelve years old. I had planted the shady side of our house with ferns, bulbs, and some lovely blue lobelia. I was quite the smug adolescent, as my own private garden was more beautiful and better maintained than the rest of the landscaping around my parents' house. (My folks were into raising children, not plants, and were kept busy producing new varieties of offspring.) I kept every weed out of my garden and worried over every chewed leaf or blighted blossom.

Since I preferred to spend my babysitting money on plants, not slug bait, I was brainstorming one day on a cheap way to kill slugs. Slugs multiply rapidly in the shady gardens of the Northwest, and I had grown tired of picking them by hand. I was collecting the slugs in a coffee can and sprinkling them with salt, when it suddenly occurred to me that salt was the answer to my slug problems.

I bought a bag of rock salt (cheaper than a bag of slug bait) and sprinkled it confidently around every plant in my precious garden. I even poured rock salt into the pots I had filled with annual flowers. I had once observed how a slug could climb up the side of a pot to feast on my flowers.

I listened to the rain fall that night and smiled to myself. I knew that the slugs were active in wet weather, and I pictured an army of slugs crawling toward a salty death in that rainstorm.

What I saw the next day was death all right — the death of every single plant in my garden. From the maidenhair ferns to the lovely lobelias, the salt treatment had dried up everything it was supposed to protect.

It wasn't until a few years later, in high school chemistry class, that I learned about salt dehydration and fully understood why an excess of salt in the soil would suck the life out of plants. By that time I had recovered from the loss and replanted the garden. I also went back to hand-picking the slugs.

Moral of the Story:
Salt and soil don't mix. Be careful when using salt to melt ice from sidewalks and pathways. And never experiment with any treatment on the entire garden. Try any new idea on one or two plants first.

The Footprints of Death

This happened to a gentlemen we'll call Herb. He had used a chemical weed killer to eliminate some blackberry bushes. The poor guy measured everything out very carefully and then aimed his poisonous spray at the offensive brambles. The blackberries just had to go because they threatened to creep into his practically perfect, emerald green lawn. (Herb admits to being a lawn fanatic.)

One suggestion Herb followed from the label was to lay cardboard on top of the nearby lawn in this area to protect it from the drift of the herbicide spray. His fatal mistake was stepping forward onto the cardboard to get closer to the enemy weeds. The soles of his shoes absorbed the poison that had drifted to the cardboard, and, as he returned to the house, he walked right across his lawn.

A couple of days passed, and then the footsteps of death began to appear. Each day they darkened, until finally, by the time the blackberry bushes had wilted, the lawn had an eerie new look. Ten patches of dead brown grass, each in the perfect outline of the owner's shoe.

Moral of the Story:
If you insist on using chemical fertilizers and weed killers, do so with caution. Be

careful where you rinse out the spray equipment, where you measure, and where you step.

Every Pruner's Pitfall

This is a story with many different versions. One woman did it to her lilac. Another couple was guilty of doing it to their azaleas, and a third party did it to the daphne. The "it" is pruning. The pitfall is pruning at the wrong time of year. Some shrubs will not bloom if you prune them improperly. Most often this happens with spring-blooming shrubs like azaleas, lilacs, and daphne. The flower buds are all formed and ready to burst forth with spring, until, one warm day in March, a garden neatnick comes along and "tidies up" the poor things.

A heavy pruning in early spring is like performing a blossom abortion on spring-blooming shrubs.

Moral of the Story:
Prune spring-flowering shrubs immediately after they bloom. Fall-blooming shrubs should be pruned in the spring, so they can use the summer months for forming flowers. Lazy gardeners will be happy to hear that too much tidying up can be tragic.

Baffled by Bloomless Bulbs

I think every gardener must have done this at least once. Even experienced gardeners that know better try it. I'm talking about cutting back the dying foliage of blooming bulbs.

One enterprising fellow (whom we'll call Bud), planted several hundred tulip bulbs and enjoyed a spring garden of intense beauty. Once spring had sprung, this neat and orderly gardener waited a few weeks for the leftover leaves of the tulips and daffodils to turn yellow and fall off. Unfortunately, it can take months for the foliage to fade away. For impatient Bud, the overripe look was just too much, and one day he snipped off every fading tulip and daffodil leaf to the ground. Bud wasted no time filling up the space with blooming annuals.

The following spring, there were thin green shoots coming up all over the yard, but not one of the tulip bulbs bloomed again. A couple of timid-looking daffodils did bloom, but only because they had been hiding from Bud's pruning shears. Hundreds of bulbs destroyed because tidiness won out over laziness.

Moral of the Story:
Don't nip off your tulip and daffodil leaves when they're yellow. You have to really let them ripen. Move them carefully to an out-of-the-way spot, or plant them where

you won't mind the mess, at a distance from the house. Lazy gardeners who don't want to replant bulbs each fall must leave them alone in the spring.

The Case of the Gray Lawn

Here's a tragic story you can see for yourself being played out on lawns across America. Lawns turn gray, not from old age, but from overfertilizing with chemical lawn foods. Applying lawn food in uneven streaks looks just as bad.

Since we switched to slow-release organic fertilizers, our lawn-feeding mistakes have been less noticeable, but there were some springs that our lawn had more stripes than a football field. Part of our problem was that we used a push-type drop lawn spreader. You have to walk carefully when you use a drop spreader, because the fertilizer spills out and drops straight down. If you overlap, you get a double dose of fertilizer and dark green streaks running down the lawn or gray dead lines where the fertilizer burned. We solved the streaking problem by switching to a broadcast spreader, which throws the fertilizer across the lawn in a more random fashion.

The worst case of an overfertilized lawn belonged to a lawn fanatic we'll call Mr. Black. He lived on a very well-traveled street. Mr. Black decided that his grass would be the greenest on the block, so he bought himself two bags of fertilizer and applied double the recommended dosage. His grass turned gray almost overnight. Not only was the lawn ruined, but the soil was so saturated from the chemical fertilizer that it took almost a full year for the ground to recover so that new seed could be planted.

Mr. Black had burned his lawn gray.

Moral of the Story:
Never use more fertilizer than the package recommends. Fertilizers are toxic in strong doses. Apply lawn foods with a broadcast spreader to avoid streaks.

The Case of the Strangled Fruit Tree

Once upon a time, a lady named Mrs. Bostonian wrote to me about her apple tree. It simply would not bear fruit, she said, and Mrs. Bostonian went on to list all the things she had tried, from fertilizing to pollinating, pruning, spraying, and pinching. The reason she was so devoted to the tree was that it had been planted by her dear husband, who passed away before he could enjoy the fruits of his labor.

I suggested more sun, more time, and more information, and finally Mrs. Bostonian convinced me to pay a yard call to see if I could tell her why the apple tree grew sicker each year.

It was a sad sight that greeted me in Mrs. Bostonian's backyard. One sick tree, as forlorn and weak as the widow herself. But, as I took a closer look, I could see the poor thing was being strangled! (The tree, not Mrs. Bostonian.) A wire was girdling the tree, cutting deep into the bark in a chokehold of death. That wire had been used by Mr. Bostonian on the first day of planting to keep the tree securely fastened to a stake for support. The supporting stake had been removed, but the wire had not, and now it was a noose around the trunk of that tree.

I wish this story had a happy ending, but unfortunately the tree died. Mrs. Bostonian didn't, however, and she wrote me again to say she was moving to a retirement complex and would only have to worry about houseplants.

Moral of the Story:
Don't wrap wire or rope around the trunks of trees or shrubs. Plastic strips torn from a heavy-duty garbage bag are safer ties to use for supporting plants.

Lips That Gave the Kiss of Death

The lips in this story are the lips or rims of the paper fiber pots that some plants are sold in at the nursery. This deathly event happened to a very nice couple we'll call Mr. and Mrs. Sahara.

The Saharas bought a new home with no landscaping. They took their time and chose a wonderful variety of plant material, placing an order with a local nursery. Now this nursery sold container-grown shrubs and used the cardboard-like fiber pots to hold their stock. Mr. and Mrs. Sahara had all their plants delivered in these pots. The truck driver reminded the young couple that they could plant the pot and all when they buried their new plants in the soil. It was hot and dry that summer, and Mr. and Mrs. Sahara were glad to hear that they wouldn't have to knock every plant from its pot and expose its roots in such heat.

A few weeks after everything was planted, the shrubs began to dry up. First the tip growth of the new plants began to die, and then the brown death spread throughout the plants. The Saharas were upset, to say the least, but they had nobody to blame except the dry weather and the way they had planted those plants.

Every pot had been sunk into the ground, but the lips of those paper fiber pots had been left above ground level, exposed to the drying sun. The Saharas had intended to bring in a bark mulch to cover up the exposed pot rims, but had blown a wad on the plants and couldn't afford to spend anything more on landscaping for awhile. Sad to say, they waited a little too long. The exposed lips of those pots acted like a wick to draw the moisture right out of the ground, and, once dry, the soil mixture was difficult to saturate again. Combine this with the fact that this couple thought they could water lightly with a hose a couple of times a week, and you have a very dry and deadly situation. Container-grown plants with crowded roots often need watering twice a day, and Mr. and Mrs. Sahara had no idea that their new plants were such big drinkers.

In the end, I think they were able to save half the shrubs, but they spent many hours and wasted many gallons of water trying to return moisture to the dried-out roots.

Moral of the Story:
Plants in pots need frequent watering, and, unless you sink the lip of the pot below the soil, you must still water as often as you would a potted plant. Also remember to water deep and long, so that the soil is thoroughly saturated. Large shrubs and trees don't appreciate being teased with a few sprinkles of moisture from a watering can.

The Row of Murdered Marigolds

My neighbor and I went to a local greenhouse and came back with our station wagon filled with marigold plants. I had talked Lilly, my flower-loving, but inexperienced, friend into planting marigolds in her sunny front yard. They were goof-proof, I promised her, and would bloom all summer long if she watered them.

Since soil in that neighborhood was very poor, I mentioned that Lilly might need to add some fertilizer to the soil to help her marigolds along. I always added peat moss and steer manure when planting my annuals, but Lilly bought a box of granular flower fertilizer, the type you sprinkle into the soil.

The morning after Lilly and I planted our mass of marigolds, her plants looked a little wilted. I checked the soil, and it was moist, so I decided I must be imagining the problem. Days passed, and Lilly grew depressed. My marigolds were taking off and starting to bloom, while hers grew sicker every day, browning from the tips inward as the wilt steadily grew worse. I just wouldn't believe her marigold murders were due to the fact that she had a black thumb. The only difference between the two beds of marigolds was the soil. She must have done something horrible to her soil, and I interrogated Lilly until the truth came out. Lilly had poured fertilizer into each little hole and then set the marigold directly on top of the granular fertilizer. She had burned the roots of those marigolds. Another case of murder by fertilizer burn.

Moral of the Story:
When using granular fertilizers, be sure to mix them thoroughly into the soil or apply them on the sides of the plant as the directions instruct. Don't set a plant on top of a pile of fertilizer.

If you've gardened at all, you probably have your own horror stories to add to this collection. I left out the very common mistakes, such as overplanting with shrubs that soon grow so tall they block the light from the windows, and adding gigantic shade trees to tiny front yards. I failed to mention all the problems people have had with certain groundcovers they forgot to prune, which soon take over the yard, or with runaway vines that try to break into the house through the windows. I didn't tell about willow roots tangling up septic tanks or birch trees dripping sticky dew all over nearby automobiles.

I certainly don't want to scare anyone away from gardening, no matter how lazy or ignorant they feel. Gardening is a game, an adventure, and you'll lose once in awhile, but win so much more.

Gardening can be challenging without being competitive, and it's good for your health, your outlook, and the market value of your home. Gardeners can be perfectionists or be laid-back — even downright lazy — and still have a lovely landscape to come home to.

Source Guide

Here's a partial list of mail-order suppliers that offer catalogs to help you find and order the plants and products that lazy gardeners love. Frugal gardeners will also find these catalogs appealing — they're all free!

Ringer Co. Natural Lawn and Garden Products
9959 Valley View Road
Eden Prairie, MN 55344-3585
(800) 654-1047

This company carries "Lawn Restore," the lawn food that improves your soil. They also offer some great watering gadgets for the lazy gardener, along with weed killers, moss killers, insecticides, and fungicides for the organic gardener.

Jackson & Perkins Co.
One Rose Lane
Medford, OR 97501-0303
(503) 776-2400

I always get a kick out of their address. Jackson & Perkins offers reliable floribunda and miniature roses, as well as many disease-resistant hybrid teas. You can also order daylilies and a few other perennials, trees, and shrubs.

Wayside Gardens
Hodges, SC 29695-0001
(800) 845-1124

Wayside calls its mailing "The Complete Garden Catalog," and I have to agree. You can order almost every tree, shrub, and flower that I can think of for the lazy gardener from Wayside. The color photographs in this catalog make it valuable as a resource guide. Every beginning gardener needs a copy for identification as well as inspiration. Hardy dwarf geraniums and the tetraploid daylilies are just two of the perennials offered that I highly recommend — and they're hard to find anywhere else.

Park Seed Co.
Flowers, Vegetables, and Bulbs
Cokesbury Road
Greenwood, SC 29647-0001
(800) 845-3369

This big company offers seeds and a lot more. You can also order soil, pots, and lights to get your seeds started. Be forewarned, though, that there are lots of luscious pictures in this catalog: You might just fall in love with a fussy, demanding flower and struggle all summer to get it to bloom.

The real beauty here is that we're talking about seeds, so every gardener can afford to experiment and search for a new favorite garden bloomer. This company sells both old-fashioned and newfangled seeds.

Get on Park's mailing list and you'll also be able to order bulbs from their fall flower book. Species tulips, grape hyacinths, and dwarf daffodils are all featured, along with the more spectacular bulb varieties that are worth the extra effort.

Gurney Seed and Nursery Co.
110 Capitol Street
Yankton, SD 57079
(605) 665-4451

Where else can you order catnip, tobacco, and money plant all from the same page? There's a lot of fun and bragging in the plant descriptions, but Gurney is a practical company that sells flowering shurbs grouped by size. Need a short-growing ornamental shrub or a shrub to use in a hedge? You get pictures and descriptions of plants that fit the need rather than nursery stock listed alphabetically. Some real bargain prices can be found in this catalog.

Index